T0316973

The Single-Period Inventory Model with Spectral Risk Measures

Forschungsergebnisse der Wirtschaftsuniversität Wien

WIRTSCHAFTS
UNIVERSITÄT
WIEN VIENNA
UNIVERSITY OF
ECONOMICS
AND BUSINESS

Band 49

PETER LANG

Frankfurt am Main · Berlin · Bern · Bruxelles · New York · Oxford · Wien

JOHANNES FICHTINGER

The Single-Period Inventory Model with Spectral Risk Measures

PETER LANG
Internationaler Verlag der Wissenschaften

Bibliographic Information published by the Deutsche Nationalbibliothek
The Deutsche Nationalbibliothek lists this publication in the Deutsche Nationalbibliografie; detailed bibliographic data is available in the internet at http://dnb.d-nb.de.

Sponsored by the Vienna University
of Economics and Business.

Cover design:
Atelier Platen according to a design of
Werner Weißhappl.

University logo of the Vienna University
of Economics and Business.
Printed with kind permission of the University.

ISSN 1613-3056
ISBN 978-3-631-61573-7
© Peter Lang GmbH
Internationaler Verlag der Wissenschaften
Frankfurt am Main 2011
All rights reserved.

www.peterlang.de

Contents

List of Figures

Chapter 1

Introduction and Foundations

Inventory management and pricing decisions based on quantitative models both in industrial practice and academic works often rely on minimizing expected cost or maximizing expected revenues or profits, which refers to the concept of risk-neutrality of the decision maker. Although many useful insights in operational problems can be obtained by such an approach, it is well understood that incorporating attitudes toward risk is an important lever for building new theories in other fields, such as economics and finance. To give an example, modern portfolio theory in finance relies heavily on consideration of risk attitudes. The level of dispersion associated with an investment might be as important as the expected gain from the investment. Hence, it is necessary to find appropriate measures of risk and the appropriate objectives related to or including these risk measures.

In operations management, inventory and pricing problems especially share commonalities with the fields mentioned above. In particular, decisions have to be taken in a stochastic environment and the policy affects the risk associated with the resulting outcome. Inventory problems of their nature can be considered similar to investment problems in finance. Hence, it is important to include risk preferences in such decision problems. Moreover, this importance is supported by recent empirical findings.

In an experimental study, Schweitzer and Cachon (2000) show that for high-profit products the ordering decisions reflect risk aversion. Similarly, through an experimental newsvendor setting, Brown and Tang (2006) show that the subjects tend to order less than the expected profit-maximizing quantity because they are concerned about potential profit loss or probability of making an acceptable profit.

Besides the risk aversion of the decision makers, using expected profit as the objective implies an analytical assumption. "In many cases, the use of the expected value as an objective can be justified by the law of large numbers: if the process is repeated, the arithmetic average of the observed profits will approach the expectation." (Collins, 2004). Specific to inventory problems, when the ordering decision is repeated many times under the very same conditions, using expected profit as the objective function can be justified. However, "if the decision is not frequently repeated or if the outcome is large relative to wealth optimizing the expectation would not be the appropriate objective for a risk-averse individual." (Collins, 2004).

Following these arguments, research on risk-averse inventory models, in particular the well-known newsvendor model with different objective functions to reflect risk preferences, has become an important stream. For example, Eeckhoudt et al. (1995) uses the concept of the expected utility framework by modifying profit realizations with a concave increasing utility function and Lau (1980) maximizes the probability of achieving a profit target.

After the axiomatic foundation of coherent risk measures by Artzner et al. (1999) the application of risk measures to inventory models became popular. For example, in an early draft, Chen et al. (2004) uses the conditional Value-at-Risk as objective and Jammernegg and Kischka (2007) proposes a convex combination of low and high profits, which can be interpreted as a mean-deviation rule. In these works results about optimal policies and structural properties are described.

However, the different risk measures are special cases of the general class of spectral risk measures introduced by Acerbi (2002). In our work we apply the spectral risk measures to the inventory control and the inventory control & pricing problem and derive optimal policies as well as structural properties. By doing so we are able to unify the results obtained so far in the literature under the common concept of spectral risk measures.

In the following section we introduce the newsvendor model and present the main properties and results of the risk-neutral problem for both the inventory and inventory & pricing problems.

1.1 The Newsvendor Model

The newsvendor model is a famous problem and building block of quantitative inventory management. It is applicable for products with short life cycles which become obsolete at the end of the period and cannot be stocked in order to satisfy any demand during the next periods. Fashion apparel retailers who must submit orders in advance of a selling season with no further opportunity for replenishment, manufacturers who have to choose the capacity before launch of a new product which will quickly become obsolete, or managers who have to decide on a special one-time promotion typically face the newsvendor problem. It also has wide applicability in service industries such as airlines and hotels where the key decision is capacity which cannot be stored and the product is generally perishable. The tendency towards short product life cycles and the growing share of service industries implies/supports the continuing interest in the newsvendor problem.

1.1.1 The inventory problem

The classical single-period, single-item, linear cost inventory control problem – the well-known newsvendor problem – is to decide on the ordering quantity before market demand is known, so that at the time of ordering demand is uncertain. The purchase cost per unit is c, and the product is sold to customers at a unit price p, which is set exogenously in the classical price-taking problem. Unsold copies be can returned to the supplier at a price v. To avoid trivial problem instances, it is generally assumed that $0 < c \leq p$ and $v < c$ holds.

If demand D, i. e. the quantity that the newsboy would be able to sell on a certain day, turns out to be equal to or greater than the ordered quantity y, then he makes a profit $\Pi(y, D)$[1] of $(p - c)y$. In the case that $D < y$ the newsvendor makes a profit of $pD + v(y - D) - cy$.

So, for a given order quantity y, the newsvendor's profit $\Pi(y)$ can be written as

$$\Pi(y) = p\min(D, y) - cy + v(y - D)^+ = (p - c)y - (p - v)(y - D)^+. \quad (1.1)$$

The objective in classical inventory models, i. e. models assuming a *risk-neutral* decision maker, is to maximize expected profit $\mathbb{E}\,\Pi(y)$, where we define $\mathbb{E}$ as the expectation operator. If demand D were known at the time of ordering, it is easy to see that the optimal decision for the newsvendor would be to order $y^* = D$, since the function $\Pi(y)$ is a continuous piecewise linear function increasing up to $y = D$ and decreasing afterwards. However, since demand is not known at the time of ordering, the problem becomes more difficult.

The demand D has to be understood as a random variable with a known demand distribution. In fact, since for real problems the exact demand distribution cannot be known either, it has to be well estimated based on collected random observations from the past. Demand can then be described by its corresponding cumulative distribution function (cdf) $F(x) := \mathbb{P}(D \leq x)$ and probability density function (pdf) $f(x)$. Since demand cannot be negative, clearly $F(x) = 0$ for any $x < 0$.

---

[1] In the following we will omit the second argument of profit and write $\Pi(y)$ keeping in mind the dependency of profit on demand.

Since the average profit tends to the expected profit if the newsvendor continues his business for a long period of time, from a statistical point of view it makes sense to optimize the expected value $\mathbb{E}\,\Pi(y)$. Note that for simplicity y is considered as a continuous rather than integer variable, which can be justified if the order quantity is reasonably large. Hence, the optimization problem can be formulated as

$$\max_{y} \mathbb{E}\,\Pi(y), \tag{1.2}$$

where

$$\mathbb{E}\,\Pi(y) = \int_0^y (px + v(y-x) - cy)\,dF(x) + \int_y^\infty (p-c)y\,dF(x).$$

Using integration by parts it is possible to reformulate this as

$$\mathbb{E}\,\Pi(y) = (p-c)y - (p-v)\int_0^y F(x)\,dx. \tag{1.3}$$

The function $\mathbb{E}\,\Pi(y)$ is concave in y with a first derivative

$$\frac{d}{dy}\mathbb{E}\,\Pi(y) = p - c - (p-v)F(y).$$

Now let $F^{-1}(\omega)$ be the inverse function of cdf F, which is defined for $\omega \in [0,1)$. Because $v < c < p$ it follows that $0 < (p-c)/(p-v) < 1$ and the optimal solution to (1.2) is

$$y^*(p) = \arg\max_{y\in\mathbb{R}^+} \mathbb{E}\,\Pi(y) = F^{-1}\left(\frac{p-c}{p-v}\right). \tag{1.4}$$

A more general, alternative problem formulation to (1.3), which can be commonly found in the literature, is defining marginal overage and underage cost of the order quantity. Overage cost c_o is the realized cost of ordering *one* unit too much when demand was lower than the order quantity, while underage cost c_u reflects the realized cost of ordering *one* unit too few for the case demand was higher than the order quantity (see e. g. Cachon and Terwiesch, 2006, for several examples).

In this work, however, we write the problem in terms of price p, cost c, salvage value v, and a non-negative shortage penalty cost s, explicitly, and do not use the model formulation based on underage and overage cost, mainly because of notational simplicity. While the case where overage cost occur is fully equivalent with our formulation (let $v = c - c_o$), the situation with shortages needs some additional consideration.

The formulation based on overage and underage cost is more general than our model assumptions as it allows to consider *lost-sales* as well as *backordering* business environments. Operating in a lost-sales business means that in a stockout situation at least the full profit margin of the product is lost. As an example, we can think of a customer entering a retailer where a certain product is out of stock. The customer does not postpone his purchase until the product is replenished but buys the product from a competitor or refrains from buying the product at all. The underage cost refers to profit margin, possibly plus some additional shortage penalties, so $c_u \geq p - c$. This case is fully considered by our model by letting $s = c_u - (p - c) \geq 0$.

The backordering case, however, refers to a business where the profit margin is not (completely) lost in a stockout situation; the customer still buys the product. However, the customer might ask for some discounts to accept late delivery, or the retailer might face higher cost due to express deliveries, etc., so underage cost might not be zero. In the backordering case the relation $0 \leq c_u < p - c$ holds, which implies $s = c_u - (p - c) < 0$. In the following analysis we are not considering this case as we assume $s \geq 0$.

Now we are ready to extend (1.1) by shortage penalty cost and define our objective function for the risk-neutral decision maker. In the following, we also derive the optimal order quantity.

Definition 1 (Profit function of a risk-neutral decision maker). *Let p, c, v and s be the retail price (marginal revenue), product cost, salvage value and shortage penalty cost, where $p > c > v$ and $v, s \geq 0$. Random demand D has a known distribution with cdf F and density f. The resulting profit $\Pi(y)$ is*

$$\Pi(y) = (p - c)D - (c - v)(y - D)^+ - (p - c + s)(D - y)^+. \qquad (1.5)$$

A risk-neutral decision maker will maximize expected profit $\mathbb{E}\,\Pi(y)$ by optimizing the order quantity y. This leads us to the following

Proposition 1 (Optimal order quantity for a risk-neutral decision maker). *The optimal order quantity y^* for a risk-neutral decision maker is*

$$y^* = \arg\max_{y \in \mathbb{R}^+} \mathbb{E}\,\Pi(y) = F^{-1}\left(\frac{p - c + s}{p - v + s}\right). \qquad (1.6)$$

Proof. Using (1.5), the expected profit is

$$\mathbb{E}\,\Pi(y) = (p-c)\,\mathbb{E}\,D - (c-v)\int_0^y (y-x)f(x)\,dx - (p-c+s)\int_y^\infty (y-x)f(x)\,dx.$$

Taking the derivative, equating to zero and solving for y leads to the well-known critical fractile solution

$$\frac{d}{dy}\,\mathbb{E}\,\Pi(y) = -(c-v)\int_0^y f(x)\,dx + (p-c+s)\int_y^\infty f(x)\,dx$$

by Leibnitz' rule

$$\frac{d}{dy}\,\mathbb{E}\,\Pi(y) = -(c-v)F(y) + (p-c+s)\Big(1 - F(y)\Big). \quad \text{Hence,}$$

$$F(y^*) = \frac{p-c+s}{p-v+s} \quad \text{and}$$

$$y^* = F^{-1}\left(\frac{p-c+s}{p-v+s}\right).$$

$\square$

Important performance measures for a newsvendor from a customer's perspective are service levels, in particular the cycle service level (CSL) and the fill rate (FR). The CSL is defined as the probability that no stockout during the selling season occurs. Sometimes called in-stock probability, it is the probability of having satisfied all demand, so the firm had stock available for each customer (Cachon and Terwiesch, 2006). This occurs if demand is not larger than the order quantity y, so

$$CSL = \mathbb{P}(D \le y) = F(y). \tag{1.7}$$

The fill rate defined as

$$FR = \mathbb{E}\,\frac{\min(D,y)}{D} \tag{1.8}$$

is the expected fraction of demand satisfied. We note here that $FR = \frac{\mathbb{E}\min(D,y)}{\mathbb{E}\,D}$ can be found commonly in the literature as approximation of the fill rate (see for example in Tempelmeier, 2005).

While service levels imply customer (external) orientation as a performance measure, the probability of missing a certain profit target level PL_L is an internally oriented performance measure for the inventory problem. It can be defined as the probability that profit stays below a given level L. For example, in some managerial situations it might be important to reach a certain target or budgeted profit level L, but any overachievement does not significantly increase utility. The performance measure PL_L now expresses the probability that this profit target level could not be reached. We can define the probability of missing a profit level L as

$$PL_L := \mathbb{P}(\Pi \leq L) \qquad (1.9)$$

where in the special case $L = 0$ the probability of any negative profit realization is considered (cf. Jammernegg and Kischka, 2007, Lau, 1980).

Further extensions to the model can be found for example in the review of Khouja (1999), and a comprehensive presentation of the single period problem in general can be found, for example, in Porteus (1990).

1.1.2 The inventory & pricing problem

When price is a decision variable[2], single period models turn into extended newsvendor problems. In addition to the ordering quantity, an optimal price is set to be charged during the period. The resulting model is now more complex because of the optimization of two variables.

The need to consider pricing and inventory problems simultaneously was first discussed by Whitin (1955). He provides a newsvendor model with pricing where a stochastic price-dependent demand function is assumed. He derives an optimality condition which equates the expected loss from not selling a marginal unit with the expected profit from selling the marginal unit.

One of the most important issues in joint pricing and inventory models is how to include uncertainty in the models. The common practice is to represent the demand function as a combination of a deterministic function and an error term. $d(p)$ is a deterministic decreasing function of price and E is a random variable with distribution function $F_E(\varepsilon)$. Two typical approaches are to combine the two terms in an additive or a multiplicative fashion. In additive models, demand is represented as the sum of the deterministic

---

[2]Note that we will discuss the pricing related aspects from an inventory control point of view. This generally means that we consider simplified price-demand response functions, while in the (empirical) marketing literature more sophisticated response functions are used.

price dependent function and the random term, i. e. $D(p) = d(p) + E$. The corresponding expected profit is

$$\Pi(p, y) = (p - c)y - (p - v) \int_{-\infty}^{y - d(p)} \Big(y - (d(p) + \varepsilon)\Big) d\,F_E(\varepsilon). \qquad (1.10)$$

In multiplicative models, demand is the product of the two terms, i. e. $D(p) = d(p)E$, and expected profit is

$$\Pi(p, y) = (p - c)y - (p - v) \int_{0}^{y/d(p)} \Big(y - (d(p)\varepsilon)\Big) d\,F_E(\varepsilon). \qquad (1.11)$$

In the additive case, the mean value of the random term is generally assumed to be zero, and in the multiplicative case it is assumed to be one. Thus, for both cases, expected demand corresponds to the deterministic part, $\mathbb{E}\,D(p) = d(p)$. It is common to assume $d(p) = a - bp$ with $a > 0$, $b > 0$ in the additive models, and $d(p) = ap^{-b}$ with $a > 0$, $b > 1$ in the multiplicative models (Petruzzi and Dada, 1999). It is also possible to consider any general function as long as it is decreasing in p.

Mills (1959) was the first to write the demand function explicitly as an additive demand model: $D(p) = d(p) + E$. The main consideration is to show the effect of uncertainty on the optimal price. For the constant marginal cost case optimal price under uncertainty is always smaller than that under certainty, but optimal ordering quantity can move in either directions. When marginal cost is increasing or decreasing optimal price may change in both directions depending on the shape of the demand curve.

Karlin and Carr (1962) also study a single period model similar to Mills (1959). However, they introduce the uncertainty in a multiplicative manner i. e. $D(p) = d(p)E$. Under this condition, the result is opposite of that under additive uncertainty. Under multiplicative uncertainty the optimal price is higher than the price under the assumption of deterministic demand. The main difference between additive and multiplicative models is the relation of price to the variance and coefficient of variation of demand. Under the additive model, while the coefficient of variation increases in price, the demand variance is constant. Under the multiplicative demand model, the coefficient of variation of demand equals that of the random term, which is independent of price, but the variance of demand is decreasing in price.

Young (1978) defined the demand function in a manner that combines both additive and multiplicative models, i. e. $D(p) = d_1(p)E + d_2(p)$. When $d_1(p) = 1$, the formulation corresponds to the additive case, and when

$d_2(p) = 0$, it corresponds to the multiplicative case. Young (1978) verifies both results of Mills (1959) and Karlin and Carr (1962), and generalizes their results by describing the optimality conditions in terms of variance and coefficient of variation. However, she does not provide an explanation about the contradicting results of additive and multiplicative cases.

Petruzzi and Dada (1999) try a more integrated framework in order to provide a possible explanation of this conflict. The idea is that price is a measure to decrease the variance and coefficient of variation of demand, but it works differently for additive and multiplicative models. In the former case, "it is possible to decrease the demand coefficient of variation without adversely affecting the demand variance by choosing a lower price"; for the latter case, on the other hand, "it is possible to decrease demand variance without adversely affecting the demand coefficient of variation by choosing a higher price". As a result, it is intuitive that the optimal price should be lower than the deterministic price in the additive model and higher in the multiplicative model.

Throughout the analysis, they use a transformation of the profit function by defining a safety factor z, and describe the optimal price as a function of z. For the additive case $z = y - d(p)$, and for the multiplicative case $z = y/d(p)$. If the realization of the random term, ε, turns out to be greater than u then shortages occur, where s is the shortage cost per unit of unsatisfied demand. If ε is less than u, leftovers occur.

Using a sequential approach, they first write the optimum price p^* as a function of z, and solve the objective function for the optimal stocking factor z^*. They find the corresponding optimal price p^* and optimal ordering quantity as $y^* = d(p^*) + z^*$ for the additive case and $y^* = d(p^*)z^*$ for the multiplicative case.

Yao et al. (2006) present the most general assumptions for the multiplicative and the additive models. They employ two important concepts: the price elasticity of demand and the generalized failure rate. They assume that the deterministic demand function has increasing price elasticity and that the error term has strictly increasing failure rate. Under these conditions they show that for both the additive and the multiplicative models the optimal policy is unique.

While the literature is dominated by the additive and the multiplicative uncertainty models, there are a small number of papers in which different demand models are analyzed under different approaches. Polatoglu (1991) studies a model without any assumptions on the structure of the demand-price relation and the inclusion of uncertainty. The distribution function of random demand $D(p)$ is defined as a general price dependent function

$F(p, x)$. Existence and uniqueness of the optimal policy constitute the focus of the study. Kocabıyıkoğlu and Popescu (2009) study a general demand model without any assumption of additive or multiplicative structure, but they still use the classical definition, i.e. $D(p)$ represents the demand as a combination of a deterministic and a random part. However, in addition to the additive and multiplicative forms, their model is also applicable for more general structures such as $D(p) = \log(E - bp)$ or $D(p) = \exp(E - bp)$. Their main assumption is the strict concavity of the revenue function in price for any risk realization. This assumption allows them to easily show the concavity of the profit function with respect to price and ordering quantity.

Yano and Gilbert (2004), Chan et al. (2004) and Elmaghraby and Keskinocak (2003) provide comprehensive reviews on combined pricing and inventory models both in the single-period and the multi-period settings.

1.2 Terminology, definitions used and conventions

We feel it is important to discuss and clarify the definitions of some technical terms used in this work. In particular, the term "risk" needs some further discussion since no unique definition exists in the literature. In finance literature risk generally refers to a potential loss, while classical economic theory generally deals with gains, so that risk describes a situation where gains are random variables associated with a known distribution function (cf. Müller and Stoyan, 2002, p. 265). Hanisch (2006) defines as risk of a decision alternative the possibility, that an undesired realization might occur, for example a (negative) deviation of some expected outcome[3].

Hence, as the term "risk" is concerned with undesired deviations from expectation, it has to be distinguished from "dispersion", which includes deviations in any direction. Clearly, a problem without stochasticity, i.e. without any dispersion, carries no risk; however a reduction of risk does not necessarily imply a reduction of dispersion.

The risk preference, i.e. risk-averse, risk-neutral or risk-seeking behaviour, refers to the attitude of the decision maker towards randomness. In Chapter 2 we will discuss this in detail and provide a definition of these terms.

Note that the term "risk" is sometimes used in the context of decision making to differentiate between a stochastic decision problem with full

---

[3]In German: „Unter dem Risiko einer Handlungsalternative wird demgegenüber die Möglichkeit einer ‚schlechten' Realisierung, sei es eine (negative) Abweichung von der erwarteten Entwicklung, sei es ein mit einer Alternative verbundener Verlust, verstanden."

knowledge of the underlying distribution functions, *decision making under risk*, in contrast to *decision making under uncertainty* or *robust decision making*, where it is not assumed that the full distribution function is known to the decision maker (cf. Schneeweiß, 1967, or Laux, 2005). With respect to this classification our work falls into "decision making under risk" as we assume the distribution function of random demand to be known to the decision maker.

1.3 Structure of the work

In Chapter 2 we discuss the foundations of decision making under risk considering risk preferences of the decision maker for the case of general profit distributions. Since the main contributions to the field of risk management have been done in the field of finance and economics, most of the relevant and reviewed literature will come from that side. However, we will keep the later application to inventory control models in mind and discuss the literature in this light. As an example, while the finance literature deals mainly with loss distributions, we discuss the content based on profit distributions. A large part of this chapter will be dedicated to the conditional Value-at-Risk and its optimization, as well as the generalization of this measure to spectral risk measures.

The subsequent chapter discusses the single-period inventory control problem under consideration of risk preferences. We generalize results described in the literature so far by using the concept of spectral measures of risk for a newsvendor without incurring shortage penalty cost, as well as for the case of positive shortage penalty cost. A brief discussion on the application of risk-averse newsvendor models in the supply chain context finishes this chapter.

Chapter 4 analyzes the combined inventory & pricing problem with risk preferences. We derive optimality conditions and structural properties for the problem with zero shortage penalty cost and conduct a numerical study for the inventory & pricing problem with shortage penalty costs. The finally, Chapter 5 concludes the work.

Chapter 2

Risk Measurement and Optimization

Different ways of considering and modeling risk preferences exist in inventory & pricing problems. These include approaches like the expected utility framework, mean-deviation criteria, maximizing the probability of reaching a certain target profit level, or the use of explicit risk measures, e. g. the conditional Value-at-Risk as discussed later on in this chapter. In the following we will briefly discuss different ways to consider risk preferences and discuss some of their properties. We describe the use of particular risk measures such as the Value-at-Risk and the conditional Value-at-Risk, and discuss spectral risk measures for the specific purpose of modeling risk preferences within inventory & pricing problems.

Since in our analysis we deal with profit distributions rather than with loss distributions, we consider the use of risk preferences on profit. Hence, undesirable deviations from expectations come from the lower (i. e. left) tail of distributions. Note that this is different than classical (financial) risk analysis where it is mainly loss distributions that are are considered.

The main intention of this chapter is to clarify the notation and to describe theory and results needed for the subsequent analysis of the inventory & pricing problem. Clearly, we do not intend to give a complete introduction to the theory of decision making under risk. For that purpose we refer the reader to Bamberg and Coenenberg (2004), Hanisch (2006), Fischer (2004a), or Menges (1974).

2.1 Early approaches to risk measures

Early approaches of considering risk and risk preferences of the decision maker include the expected utility framework, which dates back to the works of Bernoulli (1738) and got strong support by the famous work of von Neumann and Morgenstern (1944). Shortly thereafter, Markowitz (1952) introduced an important approach to risk modeling with the portfolio theory by considering the mean and standard deviations of assets for decision making. However, using standard deviation or variance has some serious flaws, as it is a symmetric measure to risk which implies that undesired downside deviations of profit are treated the same way as desired but exceptional deviations to higher profits.

2.1.1 Expected utility theory

"It is no exaggeration to consider expected utility theory the major paradigm in decision making since the Second World War" (Schoemaker, 1982). The expected utility (EU) framework has been used successfully so far in many prescriptive, i. e. normative and descriptive, i. e. positive models in management science, and in inventory control in particular. It is not the outcome of a risky prospect which is considered as basis for decision making but a function of it transformed by a risk utility function.

To understand the main idea behind this, let us look at the well-known St. Petersburg paradox discussed by Daniel Bernoulli as early as 1738. The issue in this game is why people are willing to pay only a small amount of money for a game of infinite expected outcome. The game goes as follows: A fair coin is flipped as many times as it is necessary to produce a "head" for the first time. The payoff of the game doubles with each toss it requires to see a head. So, if it takes n tosses to produce a head, the payoff is $2, 4, 8, \ldots, 2^n$ with corresponding probabilities $1/2, 1/4, 1/8, \ldots, (1/2)^n$. The expected payoff of this game is infinite, since $\sum_{n=1}^{\infty} (1/2)^n 2^n = \infty$. However, most people are only willing to pay a small amount of money to participate in such a game. By introducing a logarithmic utility function implying diminishing increases in utility for equal increases in wealth, Bernoulli was able to show that the expected utility of the game was finite (see Schoemaker, 1982, for a proof).

While Bernoulli (1738) provides mainly a positive model to describe empirically observable behavior, von Neumann and Morgenstern (1944) introduce an axiomatic foundation for decision making under risk and, hence, are able to provide normative models for decision theory. They present simple axioms (see Bamberg and Coenenberg, 2004, for a detailed discussion) which are sufficient to guarantee that the decision maker's preference about the ordering of alternatives in a decision problem fits with the ordering by their expected utility values. The expected utility in their setting is calculated based on risk utility functions which can be empirically constructed from questions like "Which certain amount is equally attractive to you as a lottery with equal probabilities for € 10 and € 10,000?" By considering comparisons between certain amounts and lotteries, not only the diminishing value in wealth under certainty can be considered, but also the decision maker's preference towards risk. Among others, Fischer (2004b) points out very clearly the difference between value functions constructed under certainty and risk utility functions under uncertainty.

Consequently, an important concept is that of risk aversion. If a decision maker prefers any lottery less than the sure outcome of its expected value, he is said to be risk-averse. On the contrary, if the decision maker prefers the lottery to the sure outcome of its expected value, he is risk-seeking. In the special case that the decision maker is indifferent between any lottery and its expected value, he is called risk-neutral. Only in the final case can decision or optimization based directly on the expected value of the outcomes be justified. This is also an important motivation for normative risk-averse (and risk-seeking) models in the field of operations management, which will be presented and discussed in the following chapters.

Any concave increasing utility function reflects risk-averse behavior, while a convex increasing utility function reflects risk-seeking behavior. The concavity of the utility function implies that the decrease in the utility from a decrease in wealth is higher than the increase in the utility from an increase in wealth. Hence, the decision maker is more sensitive to losses than to gains.

Formally, a risk utility function $u(W)$ maps a random variable of wealth, W, into the real numbers. Arrow (1971) and Pratt (1964) propose the negative ratio of the second to the first derivative of the utility function as a measure for the degree of risk aversion, so

$$\gamma(W) := -\frac{u''(W)}{u'(W)}. \tag{2.1}$$

Depending on the change in $\gamma(W)$ with respect to W the decision maker is said to have decreasing, constant, or increasing absolute risk aversion (DARA, CARA, IARA). Note that total or final wealth, W, includes the initial wealth, w_0, and the profit from operations, i.e. $W = w_0 + \Pi$.

However, albeit its interesting properties and powerful theoretical results obtained by the use of the EU framework, the main challenge in the application remains as the specification of the decision makers utility function. Remember that the utility function represents two distinct attitudes of the decision maker: the degree of the diminishing utility in wealth and the decision maker's attitude toward risk, which are inseparable from the utility function.

An approach to circumvent this problem is to find ways to measure the risk of alternatives so that the decision maker can base his decision not only on the return of an investment, but also has a way to directly address the riskiness of the alternatives. So – as Levy (2006) points out – while the EU framework does not consider risk and return separately but takes into account the whole distribution of returns, the use of dedicated risk measures allows separation of these two aspects of decision making. Hence, in the following we will discuss different ways of assessing risk by using different explicit risk measures. The selection of an appropriate risk measure, however, is not trivial, as in a normative framework any proposed risk measure needs to be based on carefully selected axioms[1].

2.1.2 Symmetric and downside risk measures

For stochastic problems, next to the mean as the measure of location, the variance as a measure of statistical dispersion is the "classical" risk measure used to describe probability distributions. The variance of a random variable Π is defined as

$$\text{Var}(\Pi) := \mathbb{E}\left(\Pi - \mathbb{E}(\Pi)\right)^2$$

and the standard deviation, $\text{SD}(\Pi) := \sqrt{\text{Var}(\Pi)}$, are used widely as risk measures, e. g. as an important measure in finance for the portfolio theory by Markowitz (1952). Though larger variance implies higher risk, i. e. the danger of an undesirable outcome increases, at the same time the "chance" of higher than expected outcomes increases too. Hence, being a symmetric risk measure variance not only penalizes downside deviations, but also the desirable upside deviations[2]. Therefore, variance does not provide a satisfying risk measure, except for the case where the outcome distribution is close to a symmetric distribution, for example the normal distribution.

Ismail and Louderback (1979) analyze profit distributions for a firm facing stochastic demand with several alternative objective functions. They show that especially for, but not limited to, the case of positive shortage penalty cost the profit distribution can be far away from being symmetric. In their paper they conclude that the shape of profit distributions changes significantly depending on price, production cost, quantities, holding costs, shortage penalty cost, demand variance, and so on, so that "the profit variance cannot be a reasonable measure of relative risk."

---

[1]See Acerbi (2004) for a motivation to use a deductive approach based on axioms of coherency which leads to a clear and unambiguous quantitative definition of risk measures.

[2]Note that the terms "higher" and "upside deviation" are used here in the sense of "better", not necessarily larger. Hence, for the case of loss distributions, higher outcomes refer to lower loss.

A common measure for symmetricity of a probability density function is the skewness Skew(Π) defined as the third standardized moment

$$\text{Skew}(\Pi) := \frac{\mathbb{E}(\Pi - \mathbb{E}(\Pi))^3}{\text{SD}(\Pi)^3}.$$

Symmetric distributions, e. g. the normal distribution, have a skewness of zero, positive skewness refers to a fat tail on the right side, negative skewness refers to fat left tails.

As a consequence of the aforementioned drawbacks of symmetric measures, there have been several risk measures introduced which explicitly consider downside risk. These risk measures ignore positive deviations and consider only the one-sided, undesirable downside deviation from an expected outcome. This definition of risk measures is more in line with the human understanding of risk. In his empirical work, Mao (1970) finds that the perception of "riskiness" by decision makers fits with downside risk measures rather than symmetric risk measures. He concludes, "To accurately portray this attitude toward risk, we need a measure of risk which not only summarizes variability, but also distinguishes between positive and negative variations. In this respect, semivariance[3] is a better measure of risk than ordinary variance."

This allows us to formulate the following:

Definition 2 (Risk). *Let Π be any random variable, where the utility $u(\Pi)$ is monotone in the realization of Π. We define the term "risk" as a measure $\rho(\Pi)$ on Π of one-sided deviations from an arbitrarily chosen value m.*

Furthermore, we say a decision maker is

1. *"risk-averse", if his objective is the minimization of undesirable deviations from m, and*

2. *"risk-seeking", if his objective is the maximization of desirable deviations from m.*

2.1.3 Value-at-Risk (VaR)

An often-used concept for risk measurement which (implicitly) considers one sided deviations from the expectation is the Value-at-Risk (VaR$_\alpha$). The

---

[3]As a risk measure already discussed by Markowitz (1959). It is defined as the expected value of squared negative deviations of possible outcomes from a certain point m, e. g. from zero or expected value. So, $\text{SemVar}_m(\Pi) := \mathbb{E}[(\Pi - m)^-]^2$.

concept of VaR_α as a measure of risk was introduced by JP Morgan in 1994[4] and became famous after considering it as a risk measure in the 2001 proposal of the Basel Banking Supervisory Committee. Quoting Szegö (2005), VaR_α was designed and proposed to answer "the following very relevant and precise questions:

- How much one can expect to lose in one day, week, year, ... with a given probability?

- What is the percentage of the value of the investment that is at risk?"

Before further discussion, let us define VaR_α (see e. g. Rockafellar and Uryasev 2002).

Definition 3 (Value-at-Risk). *The* VaR_α *associated with a profit random variable* Π *with distribution function* F_Π *is*

$$\text{VaR}_\alpha(\Pi) = \min\{\psi | F_\Pi(\psi) \geq \alpha\}. \tag{2.2}$$

As long as F_Π is continuous and strictly increasing, there is a unique ψ satisfying (2.2). Otherwise, if the inverse distribution $F_\Pi^{-1}(\alpha)$ does not exist, F_Π has a jump such that α is in an interval of confidence levels with lead to the same VaR_α. If there exists a whole range of solutions, F_Π is constant at α for a range of profit realizations π. In this case the lower endpoint of the interval is defined as VaR_α.

Statistically, VaR_α is the α-quantile of the random variable's distribution. So, VaR_α is simply the minimum outcome of a random variable within a certain confidence interval $1 - \alpha$. Hence, using confidence intervals, it is very simple to estimate the maximum loss or the minimum profit. Thereby, the width of the confidence intervals reflects the level of risk aversion, i. e., the risk preference of the decision maker. A larger confidence interval – implying a smaller α – refers to higher levels of risk aversion.

However, VaR_α as a concept to measure risk has serious flaws. We will discuss this in more detail after a short discussion on how risk can be measured in the following section.

2.1.4 Artzner's axioms of coherency: How to measure risk

In the financial context, Artzner et al. (1999) studies market risks and discuss the measurement of those risks. In their paper, they introduce a set of four

---

[4]See e. g. Holton (2002) for the history of VaR_α with consideration of the developments in the banking and securities firms in the 20th century.

properties and call each risk measure that satisfies these properties "coherent" measures of risk. In this section we present the concept of coherent measures in the literature.

An explanation of the need for coherent risk measures is given by Szegö (2005) by relating properties of risk measures to (intuitive) properties of a measure of distance between two points:

> "We recall the three conditions that any ... [function] defining the distance between two points ... must satisfy:
>
> - the distance between a point and itself is zero;
> - the distance does not change by inverting the two points;
> - given three points, the distance between any pair cannot be larger than the sum of the distances between the other two pairs."

While all of those three properties sound intuitive and any potential measure of distance necessarily has to satisfy them, analogous conditions for risk measurement are not satisfied by many of the existing approaches, such as the VaR_α. Artzner et al. (1999) propose a set of properties that any acceptable risk measure $\rho(\Pi)$ must satisfy.

Definition 4 (Coherent measure of risk). *Let Π be any random variable and $\rho(\Pi)$ a function defining the risk of Π. The risk measure $\rho(\cdot)$ is called coherent, if and only if it satisfies the four properties*

1. *Translation equivariance: $\rho(\Pi + a) = \rho(\Pi) + a$. Adding a sure outcome of amount a to the random outcome of Π increases the risk measure by exactly this amount a.*

2. *Subadditivity: $\rho(\Pi + Z) \leq \rho(\Pi) + \rho(Z)$ for all random variables Π and Z. The risk of joint operations cannot be higher than the risk of two independent, single operations. This property implies that merely splitting up operations of a company into different independent divisions cannot reduce the total operational risk.*

3. *Positive homogeneity: $\rho(\lambda\Pi) = \lambda\rho(\Pi)$ for all random variables Π and all positive real numbers $\lambda \geq 0$.*

4. *Monotonicity: $\Pi \prec_{SD(1)} Z \Rightarrow \rho(\Pi) \geq \rho(Z)$ for all random variables Π and Z, where $\prec_{SD(1)}$ denotes stochastic dominance of order 1 so that the cumulative distribution functions (cdf) of Π and Z are ordered, $F_\Pi(z) \geq F_Z(z)$ for all z.*

Artzner et al. (1999) state that only those risk measures satisfying all of the above properties can lead to conclusive results in risk measurement. For a broader review of different risk measures with respect to Artzner's axioms see e. g. Hanisch (2006), and references therein. A discussion of VaR_α follows in the next section.

As an example, we now illustrate that variance is not a coherent measure of risk. In particular, variance does not satisfy any of the axioms stated above.

1. *Translation equivariance* is violated since

$$\text{Var}(\Pi + a) = \text{Var}(\Pi) \neq \text{Var}(\Pi) + a.$$

2. *Subadditivity* $\text{Var}(\cdot)$ is not subadditive for any correlated random variables, Π and Z:

$$\begin{aligned} \text{Var}(\Pi + Z) &= \text{Var}(\Pi) + \text{Var}(Z) + 2\text{COV}(\Pi, Z) \\ &> \text{Var}(\Pi) + \text{Var}(Z) \quad \text{for COV}(\Pi, Z) > 0. \end{aligned}$$

3. *Positive homogeneity* does not hold since

$$\text{Var}(\lambda \Pi) = \lambda^2 \, \text{Var}(\Pi) \neq \lambda \, \text{Var}(\Pi).$$

4. And finally, the *Monotonicity* property does not necessarily hold, which can be easily seen, for example, if we let $\Pi \sim \text{Unif}(0, 1)$ and $Z \sim \text{Unif}(0, 3)$, so $\Pi \prec_{SD(1)} Z$ but $\text{Var}(\Pi) < \text{Var}(Z)$.

2.1.5 VaR in view of Artzner's axioms

After the work of Artzner et al. (1999) the ability of VaR_α to measure risk in a valid way was seriously questioned (for a strong criticism see Szegö, 2005).

A major point is the definition of VaR_α as a single point in the value distribution. While its definition of the worst outcome within a certain confidence interval, e. g. 95%, sounds intuitive and helpful, Acerbi et al. (2008) state that this implies at the same time considering the best possible outcome for describing the risk associated with the worst 5% cases of a distribution. "Once we have selected these cases", Acerbi et al. (2008) raise the question, "why should we be interested in the least loss irrespectively of how serious all the other losses are?"

This issue raises problems for value distributions with fat (left) tails, which is revealing for rare events with high losses. On the contrary, for the case when the value distribution has a positive skewness, the problems mentioned above seem to be less serious.

However, analyzing Artzner's axioms, Pflug (2000) shows that VaR_α is translation equivariant, positively homogeneous and monotone, but does not necessarily satisfy the subadditivity property. This might cause the problem that a risky operation could be reduced in its risk by splitting it up into two distinct divisions. Further, risk assessment for a whole company becomes problematic since optimizing single (risky) operations with respect to the risk measure does not necessarily end up in a risk optimum for the whole organization. As an example, it is not guaranteed that, despite compliance with risk limits for each product group in a company, the total risk level is within the desired levels.

Due to these problems, VaR_α – although ostensibly easy and intuitive – does not seem to be appropriate as a risk measure for inventory-related risk, and, moreover, is particularly inappropriate once it is used as an objective function within an optimization procedure of some profit (or cost). However, there are papers proposing VaR_α for inventory control (Tapiero, 2005, uses VaR_α for inventory control, although in a slightly different setting) and even for the capacity constrained multi-product setting (as an example see Özler et al., 2009).

2.2 Conditional Value-at-Risk (CVaR)

A natural extension of VaR_α is to not only consider the α-quantile itself, but to consider the conditional expected value of this tail of the distribution, that is the mean of the $100\alpha\%$ worst realizations. The resulting measure is the so-called conditional Value-at-Risk ($CVaR_\alpha$), or as some authors refer to it, expected shortfall. Introduced by Rockafellar and Uryasev (2000), the conditional Value-at-Risk can be seen as a response to the serious conceptual problems of VaR_α. An excellent review and introduction to the concept of $CVaR_\alpha$ can be found for example in the tutorial of Sarykalin et al. (2008).

The conditional Value-at-Risk has several advantages over VaR_α:

1. It is *coherent* in the sense of Artzner's axioms (see Pflug, 2000, for a proof). In particular, $CVaR_\alpha$ satisfies the subadditivity axiom, so that it can be used for aggregating risk over several operations to a firm-wide risk measure.

2. It also takes *rare events* below $F_\Pi^{-1}(\alpha)$ into consideration. More important for the application of the risk measure, however,

3. CVaR_α can be formulated as a *maximization problem* and allows for incorporation into optimization problems on decisions y affecting the random variable of outcome $\Pi(y)$.

2.2.1 Definition of conditional Value-at-Risk

The conditional Value-at-Risk for a given confidence level α is defined as

$$\text{CVaR}_\alpha(\Pi) = \frac{1}{\alpha} \int_0^\alpha F_\Pi^{-1}(\omega) \, d\omega. \tag{2.3}$$

CVaR_α as an objective function again implies sensitivity about the lower values of profit. When $\alpha = 1$, all possible values of profit are considered, so the problem is identical to the risk-neutral problem. However, for any $\alpha < 1$, only a lower fraction of the sample space is considered. For example, $\alpha = 5\%$ implies that the decision maker only considers the 5% worst outcomes of the sample space and bases his decision or optimization on these events. Consequently, his approach implies risk aversion by optimizing outcome given that one of the 5% worst cases arose such that he cuts his losses.

Note that for the special case where the random variable has a continuous, strictly monotone increasing cdf, CVaR_α equals the conditional expected value given the outcome is below the Value-at-Risk, so

$$\text{CVaR}_\alpha(\Pi) = \mathbb{E}(\Pi | \Pi \leq \text{VaR}_\alpha(\Pi)).$$

However, in the newsvendor problem we need to consider discontinuous distribution functions of profit. In particular, as will be shown later, there is a discontinuity in the profit distribution $F_\Pi(\pi)$ at a certain value $\bar{\pi}$ such that $F_\Pi(\pi)$ is continuous and monotone increasing for all $\pi < \bar{\pi}$ and 1 for all $\pi \geq \bar{\pi}$. The problem of a discontinuity of the cdf is shown in Figure 2.1, where for a certain random variable Π, $F_\Pi(\pi) = \alpha$ does not exist. In this case the shaded area in the left plot represents the conditional expectation given $\pi \leq \text{VaR}_\alpha(\Pi)$, which does not correspond to the actual CVaR_α, which is indeed the shaded area in the right plot.

A common possibility to circumvent the problem is by rescaling the original variable Π which has a jump at $\bar{\pi}$ by α, so that we come up with a new

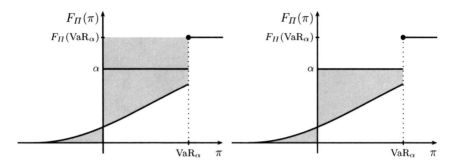

Figure 2.1: Distribution of Π where ψ such that $F_\Pi(\psi) = \alpha$ does not exist. The conditional expectation given $\pi \leq \text{VaR}_\alpha(\Pi)$ in the left plot (shaded area divided by α) does not result in the correct CVaR_α, as can be seen by comparison with the correct area in the right plot.

random variable $\bar{\Pi}$ which corresponds to the α-tail of Π. The distribution of $\bar{\Pi}$, $F_{\bar{\Pi}}$ can be defined as

$$F_{\bar{\Pi}}(\pi) = \begin{cases} \frac{F_\Pi(\pi)}{\alpha} & \text{for } \pi < \bar{\pi} \\ 1 & \text{otherwise.} \end{cases} \tag{2.4}$$

As a consequence, the conditional Value-at-Risk can easily be calculated by taking the expected value of $\bar{\Pi}$, so $\text{CVaR}_\alpha(\Pi) = \mathbb{E}(\bar{\Pi})$. The rescaling of Π to $\bar{\Pi}$ is also illustrated in Figure 2.2. As can be seen, this definition rescales the distribution by α so that instead of the original distribution between the horizontal zero-line and α-line, it forms a new distribution function between zero and one (see Rockafellar and Uryasev, 2002).

Another way to overcome the problem of the discontinuity in the cdf is to use the generalized inverse distribution function defined as $F^{-1}(\omega) := \inf\{u : u \geq \omega)$ as discussed by Pflug and Ruszczyński (2004). Let $\alpha^+ := F(F^{-1}(\alpha))$, then CVaR_α can be represented by

$$\text{CVaR}_\alpha(\Pi) = \frac{1}{\alpha} \int_0^\alpha F_\Pi^{-1}(\omega) \, d\omega$$

$$= \mathbb{E}(\Pi | \Pi \leq F_\Pi^{-1}(\alpha)) - \left(\frac{\alpha^+ - \alpha}{\alpha} \right) F_\Pi^{-1}(\alpha). \tag{2.5}$$

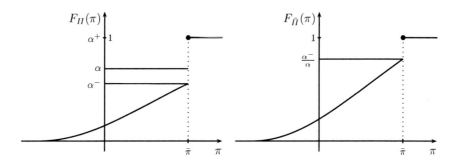

Figure 2.2: Distribution of Π where $F_\Pi(\pi) = \alpha$ does not exist (left). The rescaled distribution $F_{\bar\Pi}(\pi) = F_\Pi(\pi)/\alpha$ for $\pi < \bar\pi$ is used for further CVaR_α calculation (right).

Graphically, this refers to taking the conditional expectation as in the left plot of Figure 2.1 and subtracting the difference in the area between the left and the right plot, i.e. $(\alpha^+ - \alpha)F_\Pi^{-1}(\alpha)$, rescaled by $1/\alpha$.

For the analysis of the inventory problem later on in Chapter 3 we will use both of these approaches. For some problems, it will be convenient to rescale the demand distribution and consider this transformed distribution for the newsvendor problem. This helps us to use results obtained already in the literature on the risk-neutral newsvendor, which can then be applied to the newsvendor with a transformed distribution function.

2.2.2 Optimization of CVaR

As long as CVaR_α is used as a performance indicator, applying (2.3) is perfectly fine to calculate CVaR_α for a given sample, e.g. for realizations of a newsvendor's profit. But once we want to maximize an objective function containing CVaR_α by optimizing some control, the problem becomes a little bit more tedious. Now we have to consider two distinct cases, which we will describe in the following example.

Assume there is a newsvendor making a random profit Π and the only control available is the order quantity y. Furthermore, profit depends on random demand, D. Now, we can distinguish two cases in the relation of Π and D. In the first case the function between demand and profit is monotone, so that a higher realization of demand results in higher profit and vice versa.[5] An optimization of the order quantity y based on the $\alpha\%$-worst profit realizations can be simply done by considering the $\alpha\%$-worst demand cases only. In the second case, however, no monotone relation between demand and profit exists anymore. This is the case, for example, if our newsvendor considers penalty costs for unsatisfied demand in his objective function. Now, low profits is a result of low and high demand due to low sales in the first case and high penalties in the latter case. For the optimization on the order quantity it is no longer possible to consider a subset of demand realizations, but for each quantity the profit has to be sorted and the lowest α-fraction of it evaluated. Since the monotonicity does not hold, the optimization requires repeated resorting of profit. Consequently, for a practical application in numerical computation on a discrete set of scenarios, standard minimization algorithms implemented in software products get into troubles when trying to optimize (2.3) as an objective function due to the discrete reshuffling of scenarios as pointed out by Acerbi (2004).

Rockafellar and Uryasev (2000, 2002) and Pflug (2000) propose an elegant way to overcome the problem of sorting while optimizing. In their approach, CVaR_α is defined as the solution to a concave maximization problem over an auxiliary variable ψ.

Proposition 2 (Fundamental CVaR_α maximization formula). *Let y be the control variable of random profit $\Pi(y)$, e.g. the order quantity for a newsvendor.*

1. *The following formulation is equivalent to the definition of CVaR_α in (2.3),*

$$\text{CVaR}_\alpha(\Pi(y)) = \max_{\psi \in \mathbb{R}} \Gamma(y, \psi), \qquad (2.6)$$

where $\Gamma(y, \psi)$ is defined as

$$\Gamma(y, \psi) := \psi + \frac{1}{\alpha} \mathbb{E}(\Pi(y) - \psi)^-. \qquad (2.7)$$

2. *Maximizing $\text{CVaR}_\alpha(\Pi)$ with respect to y is equivalent to maximizing $\Gamma(y, \psi)$ over all (y, ψ) in the sense that*

$$\max_{y \in \mathbb{R}^+} \text{CVaR}_\alpha(\Pi(y)) = \max_{(y, \psi) \in \mathbb{R}^+ \times \mathbb{R}} \Gamma(y, \psi) \qquad (2.8)$$

---

[5]Note that the relation could be inverse as well, so that a higher realization of the state variable D leads to a lower realization of profit. This still refers to case 1 as the relation is still monotone.

See Rockafellar and Uryasev (2002, Theorem 10, 14) for a proof. Note that as a side effect of the optimization of CVaR$_\alpha$, the argument ψ that maximizes (2.6) corresponds to VaR$_\alpha$ (cf. Pflug, 2000). Hence, by solving the optimization problem, the optimal control to maximize CVaR$_\alpha$ and its corresponding VaR$_\alpha$ are found.

An important additional result concerns the concavity of the optimization problem, summarized in the following:

Corollary 1 (Concavity of CVaR$_\alpha$). *If $\Pi(y)$ is concave with respect to y, then* CVaR$_\alpha(\Pi(y))$ *is concave with respect to y as well. Indeed, in this case* $\Gamma(y, \psi)$ *is jointly concave in (y, ψ).*

See Rockafellar and Uryasev (2002, Corollary 11) for a proof. This result will turn out to be very useful for proofs of concavity of the profit with respect to order quantity in the following chapters.

2.3 Spectral measures of risk

The risk measures discussed in the previous sections are some special cases of a more general class of risk measures, the so-called spectral measures of risk, introduced by Acerbi (2002)[6]. To understand spectral measures, we can think of the CVaR$_\alpha$ as a weighted average of realizations of a random variable Π, where the weights are $1/\alpha$ for the worst $100\alpha\%$ outcomes and zero weights are assigned for the better outcomes.

2.3.1 Definition of spectral measures of risk

Clearly, it can be seen that this is a special case of a more general probability-weighted average in the form of

$$\mathrm{M}(\Pi) = \int_0^1 \phi(\omega) F_\Pi^{-1}(\omega) \, d\omega, \tag{2.9}$$

where the function $\phi(\omega)$ for $\omega \in [0, 1]$ allows us to specify, in general, a function of weights over the probability range and hence, indirectly, over the inverse distribution function F_Π^{-1}. We will call ϕ the *risk spectrum* of the risk measure $\mathrm{M}(\Pi)$.

Acerbi (2002) defines three conditions on the risk spectrum and shows that $\mathrm{M}(\Pi)$ is coherent if and only if ϕ satisfies these conditions:

---

[6]Note that similar definitions were made under the name of law-invariant co-monotone-additive coherent measure of risk by Kusuoka (2001).

1. *Positivity:* The risk spectrum is non-negative in its domain,

$$\phi(\omega) \geq 0 \quad \forall \, \omega \in [0,1]$$

2. *Normalization:* The risk spectrum adds up to 1,

$$\int_0^1 \phi(\omega) \, d\omega = 1$$

3. *Monotonicity:* The risk spectrum is non-increasing in its domain,

$$\phi(\omega_1) \geq \phi(\omega_2) \quad \forall \, 0 \leq \omega_1 \leq \omega_2 \leq 1.$$

Note that these conditions imply that any risk measure which neglects the leftmost end of the tail cannot be coherent, as is the case with VaR_α. Furthermore note that the risk spectrum being non-increasing makes a risk measure which puts more weight on low rather than on high outcomes. This implies risk-averse behavior of the decision maker. A risk-neutral decision maker would apply a constant risk spectrum and a risk-seeking decision maker would apply a non-decreasing risk spectrum. Important however is the fact that the risk spectrum is monotone in the probability.

In our work, we also allow the risk spectrum to be increasing (non-decreasing) in its domain to model risk-seeking behavior of the decision maker, we only require monotonicity. However, we need a forth, additional assumption, which is that the risk spectrum be finite. So, let us summarize this in the following:

Definition 5 (Admissible risk spectrum). *We call a risk spectrum $\phi(\omega)$ with $\omega \in [0,1]$ admissible, if and only if it satisfies the positivity, normalization and monotonicity criteria and, additionally, is finite for all ω.*

In the next two examples it can be seen that both CVaR_α and VaR_α are special cases of a general spectral risk measure with a particular risk spectrum. Furthermore, the risk spectrum of CVaR_α satisfies the conditions of coherency while the risk spectrum of VaR_α does not.

Example 1 (CVaR_α). From (2.9) it is easy to see that CVaR_α is a special case of a spectral risk measure with risk spectrum

$$\phi(\omega) = \begin{cases} \frac{1}{\alpha} & \omega \leq \alpha \\ 0 & \text{otherwise.} \end{cases} \tag{2.10}$$

The risk spectrum is a piecewise constant function, with a decreasing single step in $\omega = \alpha$. If we plug (2.10) in (2.9), we get (2.3) again. Note that the risk spectrum satisfies the conditions of coherency, in particular the monotonicity condition.

Example 2 (Mean-CVaR$_\alpha$). A commonly used extension of the pure CVaR$_\alpha$ formulation is a convex combination of CVaR$_\alpha$ and the expected value, which leads to a mean-CVaR$_\alpha$ formulation. This risk spectrum uses two parameters, $\alpha, \lambda \in [0,1]$.

$$\phi(\omega) = \begin{cases} \frac{\lambda}{\alpha} & \omega \leq \alpha \\ \frac{1-\lambda}{1-\alpha} & \text{otherwise.} \end{cases} \tag{2.11}$$

Again, α refers to the confidence interval of CVaR$_\alpha$, while λ defines the weight of the CVaR$_\alpha$ on the overall risk spectrum (hence $1 - \lambda$ is the weight of the expected value). Unlike the pure CVaR$_\alpha$, this risk spectrum is able to represent risk-averse, risk-neutral and risk-seeking decision making behavior. When $\lambda > \alpha$, relatively more weight is given to the lower realizations, which implies risk aversion; while for $\lambda < \alpha$ the relative weight of the lower realizations is smaller than of the others, which is risk-seeking behavior. For the special case $\lambda = \alpha$ the relative weights of lower and higher realizations are the same, hence, the decision maker is risk-neutral.

Example 3 (VaR$_\alpha$). Also VaR$_\alpha$ can be seen as a special case of (2.9). Since VaR$_\alpha$ considers one specific outcome only, in particular the best of the $\alpha\%$ worst, the risk spectrum is a positive single peak at point α. The risk spectrum is not finite and does not satisfy the monotonicity condition here, since a single peak of infinite height is the strongest possible violation of monotonicity. See Acerbi (2004) for a more formal discussion of VaR$_\alpha$ as a spectral measure.

While measuring the level of a decision maker's risk aversion is simple in the case of the CVaR$_\alpha$ (a smaller α implies a higher level of risk aversion), when using general risk spectra it is no longer that easy to compare the level of risk aversion. However, to be able to derive structural properties of the optimal solution with respect to the level of risk aversion later on, we need an objective way to assess risk aversion. In order to do so, we introduce the following:

Definition 6 (Order of risk aversion). *Let DM_1 and DM_2 be two decision makers with risk spectra ϕ_1 and ϕ_2, respectively. We call the aggregated risk spectra $\Phi_i(\omega) = \int_0^\omega \phi_i(t)\, dt$ risk transformation functions.*

1. DM_1 is called more risk-averse than DM_2 at probability ω if $\Phi_1(\omega) > \Phi_2(\omega)$.

2. Moreover, we call DM_1 strictly more risk-averse than DM_2, if (a) holds for at least one specific ω and, additionally, if $\Phi_1(\omega) \geq \Phi_2(\omega)$ holds for every $\omega \in [0,1]$.

Definition 6, concerning the ordering of risk aversion, implies that any risk-averse decision maker has a risk transformation function $\Phi(\omega) > \omega$ for all ω. The task of the risk transformation function is to transform the distribution function of the state into a "virtual" distribution of a "virtual" state where implicitly the risk preference of the decision maker is considered; see the discussion about the rescaling of the distribution function in the specific case of a $CVaR_\alpha$ decision maker in Section 2.2.1, in particular Figure 2.2 (cf. Rockafellar and Uryasev, 2002). Since for any risk-averse decision maker $\Phi^{-1}(t) < t$ holds, the risk transformation is a downward transformation of the quantile, so $F(x) < F_\phi(x)$ if $F(x)$ denotes the distribution of the state and $F_\phi(x) := \Phi\left(F(x)\right)$ the transformed distribution.

To illustrate the concept of ordering with an example, consider a risk-neutral decision maker facing a newsvendor problem as presented in (1.2), where the optimal cycle service level, i. e. the target quantile, was found to be $\frac{p-c}{p-v}$. Once the decision maker becomes risk-averse, the distribution of the state will be transformed or rescaled such that $F_\phi(x) > F(x)$ for any x, which implies that the optimal order quantity will be smaller than the risk-neutral solution (for a detailed discussion of this point see the analysis of the inventory problem in Chapter 3).

For the later analysis we need the following definition of a parameter measuring the risk preference.

Definition 7 (Parameter of risk preference). *We define η as a generic, ordinal scaled, monotone increasing parameter of the decision maker's risk preference. Further, it is normalized, such that $\eta = 1$ refers to risk neutrality, any $\eta < 1$ implies risk aversion and $\eta > 1$ risk-seeking behavior.*

Definition 7 based on Definition 6(b) introduces an ordinal scaled[7] parameter of the decision maker's risk preference. We say that the risk preference increases in η. As an example, decision maker 1 with $\eta_1 = 0.6$ has a lower risk preference than decision maker 2 with $\eta_2 = 0.8$, although both are risk-averse. A decision maker 3 with $\eta_3 = 1.2$ has a higher risk preference

---

[7]There is the restriction that η only allows power transformations as we normalize the parameter so that $\eta = 1$ refers to the risk-neutral preference.

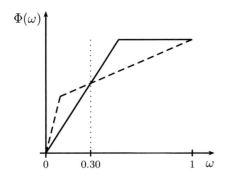

Figure 2.3: Two decision makers with different risk spectra: Decision maker DM_1 with CVaR_α risk spectrum, $\alpha = 0.5$ (solid line) compared with decision maker DM_2 using a mean-CVaR_α risk spectrum with $\alpha = 0.1$, $\lambda = 0.5$ (dashed line). While DM_2 is more risk-averse for lower probabilities (< 0.3), the pure CVaR_α decision maker DM_1 becomes more risk-averse for the higher probability ranges.

than decision maker 1 and 2, and he is risk-seeking. Note, however, that we cannot formulate a direct relation between a specific value of η and the parameters of the underlying risk-spectrum. As an example, there exists no function that maps α and λ for a mean-CVaR_α risk spectrum into η. All we can say for this example is that for any $\lambda > \alpha$, the corresponding $\eta < 1$ (risk aversion), and for any $\lambda < \alpha$, $\eta > 1$ (risk-seeking), with the special case of risk neutrality for the equality of both parameters.

This generic parameter of the risk spectrum is used later on to derive general results with respect to the level of risk preference. It allows us, independent of the underlying risk spectrum, to conduct sensitivity analysis on the problem. For example, we are able to draw conclusions such as the objective function is increasing in the risk preference, etc. When we perform numerical analysis, so when concrete risk spectra are used, we specify the corresponding parameters of the risk spectra. As an example, in numerical plots with a mean-CVaR_α risk spectrum, we specify directly α and λ, and not η.

Note that it is not always possible to strictly order the risk preferences of the decision maker. It is easy to imagine that the risk transformation functions can intersect. See Figure 2.3 for an example of two decision makers where the first one applies a pure CVaR_α risk spectrum and the other a mean-CVaR_α formulation. We will see later for the inventory problem in Chapter 3 that the ordering of the optimal decision, i.e. the optimal order quantity, for two risk-averse decision makers depends then on the target cycle service level.

2.3.2 Discussion on how to model the risk spectrum

While a risk spectrum satisfying Definition 5 can be any finite, monotone, non-negative, normalized function to guarantee coherence of the decision, little discussion has been done so far in the literature about the concrete formulation of risk spectra. Dowd et al. (2008) review some of the "natural" formulations of risk spectra, such as decreasing exponential functions and power functions, which we will use later in Chapters 3 and 4 to model the risk preferences of the decision maker for inventory and pricing problems. Sriboonchitta et al. (2009) relate classical risk utility functions to risk spectra.

Following Dowd et al. (2008), a common formulation used for risk utility functions is the power utility function. Accordingly, we can formulate a weighting function on the probabilities similar to the power utility function in the EU framework,

$$\phi(\omega) = \frac{1}{k}(1 - \omega)^{\frac{1}{k}-1}, \tag{2.12}$$

where the parameter $k \in (0, \infty)$ reflects the degree of risk-aversion of the decision maker such that higher values of k refer to higher levels of risk-aversion. It can be easily seen that for any finite k this function satisfies all properties in Definition 5. Moreover, for $k < 1$ the risk spectrum reflects risk-averse behavior, $k = 1$ refers to the risk-neutral case where ϕ is constant, and any $k > 1$ results in risk-seeking behavior. If $0.5 < k < 1$ the risk spectrum is concave, which implies a progressive marginal sensitivity on the probabilities, while for the case $k < 0.5$ the decision maker has a diminishing marginal sensitivity and the risk spectrum is convex. The case $k = 0.5$ is a special case with a linear risk spectrum. Hence, this proposed risk spectrum is quite flexible by choosing the appropriate parameter. Note, however, that $\phi(1) = 0$, which implies that the risk spectrum does not (implicitly) contain the expected value of profit. An example of a power risk spectrum is shown in Figure 2.4 (left) for different parameter values.

Another possible risk spectrum based on the exponential risk utility function is the exponential risk spectrum, defined as

$$\phi(\omega) = \frac{ue^{-u\omega}}{1 - e^{-u}}, \tag{2.13}$$

where u reflects the level of risk-aversion. For a strictly positive parameter $u > 0$, this risk spectrum also satisfies all properties in Definition 5. It (implicitly) considers a mean-risk formulation since $\phi(1) \neq 0$. Hence, the risk spectrum can be decomposed into a mean-risk formulation, where mean has a weight $\phi(1)$ and the risk part $1 - \phi(1)$. Increasing values of the parameter

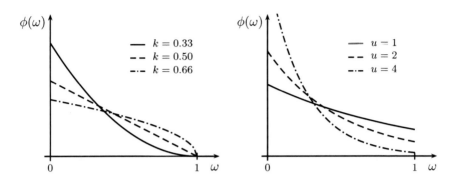

Figure 2.4: Two examples of risk spectra: Power risk spectrum $\phi(\omega) = \frac{1}{k}(1-\omega)^{\frac{1}{k}-1}$ for $k = \{0.33; 0.5; 0.67\}$ (left). Note that for such power functions any $0.5 < k < 1$ leads to a concave risk spectrum, while $k < 0.5$ results in a convex risk spectrum. A linear risk spectrum is the special case of $k = 0.5$. In the right plot, an exponential risk spectrum $\phi(\omega) = \frac{u e^{-u\omega}}{1-e^{-u}}$ for $u = \{1; 2; 4\}$ is shown.

u again increase the diminishing marginal sensitivity in probability about profit.

2.3.3 Optimization of general spectral measures of risk

With the same arguments as in the optimization of CVaR_α, the application of a spectral risk measure as a performance indicator is easily possible by using (2.9) to describe the riskiness in the desired form. Once the decision maker intends to optimize an objective function based on spectral measures, the same problem that we faced for the optimization of CVaR_α in Section 2.2.2 will come up again: the problem of resorting. Acerbi and Simonetti (2002) extend the method of Pflug/Rockafellar/Uryasev to the general spectral measure M.

Proposition 3 (Fundamental maximization formula). *Let y be the control variable of random profit $\Pi(y)$, e. g. the order quantity for a newsvendor. Let us further define a $\Gamma(y, \psi)$ such that*

$$\Gamma(y, \psi) := \phi(1)\,\mathbb{E}\,\Pi(y) - \int_0^1 \frac{d\phi}{d\omega}\left\{\omega\psi(\omega) + \mathbb{E}(\Pi(y) - \psi(\omega))^-\right\}\,d\omega. \quad (2.14)$$

1. *If the decision maker is* risk-averse, *i. e. the risk spectrum ϕ is decreasing, the following formulation is equivalent to the definition of the spectral risk measure in (2.9),*

$$\mathrm{M}(\Pi(y)) = \max_{\psi} \Gamma(y, \psi). \tag{2.15}$$

Further, maximizing $\mathrm{M}(\Pi(y))$ with respect to y is equivalent to maximizing the functional $\Gamma(y, \psi)$ over y and the function $\psi : (0, 1) \to \mathbb{R}$ in the sense that

$$\max_{y} \mathrm{M}(\Pi(y)) = \max_{(y, \psi)} \Gamma(y, \psi) \tag{2.16}$$

2. *If the decision maker is* risk-seeking, *i. e. the risk spectrum ϕ is increasing, the following formulation is equivalent to the definition of the spectral risk measure in (2.9),*

$$\mathrm{M}(\Pi(y)) = \min_{\psi} \Gamma(y, \psi). \tag{2.17}$$

See Acerbi and Simonetti (2002) for a proof.

From this formulation it is immediately clear that the sorting problem of the outcomes cannot be replaced by separating them into two subsets with a single variable ψ, as was the case with CVaR_{α}. Now each possible realization has to be distinguished from the others since it potentially carries a different weight with it. Hence, the single auxiliary variable ψ in the case of CVaR_{α}-optimization now turns into a continuous function $\psi(\omega)$ defined for $\omega \in (0, 1)$ and the maximization has to be carried out on Γ by optimizing the whole function $\psi(\omega)$.

An important additional result concerns the concavity of the optimization problem, summarized in the following:

Corollary 2 (Concavity of M). *If $\Pi(y)$ is concave with respect to y, then $\mathrm{M}(\Pi(y))$ is concave with respect to y as well. Indeed, in this case $\Gamma(y, \psi)$ is jointly concave in (y, ψ).*

See Acerbi and Simonetti (2002) for a proof. Again, this result will turn out to be very useful for proofs of concavity of the profit with respect to order quantity in the following chapters.

Although formulations (2.15) and (2.17) allow for very general definitions of risk spectra, the optimization becomes very difficult to solve in the truly continuous case. Especially to ease numerical optimization, the risk

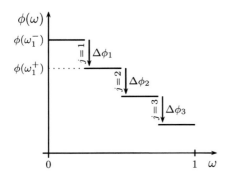

Figure 2.5: Example of a discretized risk spectrum with $J = 3$ jumps. The height of each jump j is $\Delta\phi_j < 0$. Note that the case $\phi(1) > 0$ is not considered a jump anymore.

spectrum can be discretized into a piecewise constant function with a finite number of J jumps at $\alpha = \alpha_1, \ldots, \alpha_J < 1$. The height of each jump is $\Delta\phi_j = \phi(\omega^+) - \phi(\omega^-)$ for $j = 1, \ldots, J$, where $\phi(\omega^+)$ denotes the risk spectrum at ω evaluated from the right and $\phi(\omega^-)$ is evaluated from the left. See Figure 2.5 for an illustration of a discretized risk spectrum. Note that $\Delta\phi_j < 0$ for all j implies risk aversion while the case $\Delta\phi_j > 0$ for all j implies a risk-seeking preference by the decision maker.

The discretization of the risk spectrum reduces the problem to an optimization problem of J auxiliary variables ψ_j, so $\Gamma(\Pi, \psi)$ can be written as

$$\Gamma(\Pi, \psi) = \phi(1)\,\mathbb{E}(\Pi) - \sum_{j=1}^{J} \Delta\phi_j \left\{ \omega_j \psi_j + \mathbb{E}(\Pi - \psi_j)^- \right\}. \qquad (2.18)$$

The optimization of (2.18) over the vector ψ can be again carried out with high efficiency by using standard optimization algorithms implemented in software tools.

Chapter 3

Inventory Problem with Risk Measures

While a lot of results have been obtained so far for the classical risk-neutral newsvendor problem, fewer works have considered a risk-averse or risk-seeking decision maker for the inventory problem. Early works generally cover risk preferences by applying the expected utility theory framework. Profit or losses from operations are added to the newsvendor's final wealth. A transformation of final wealth by the utility function allows a comparison of different order quantities in a relative sense, so that an optimal order quantity can be found. Structural results of these works are not always comparable because different models are considered.

A close approach to ours of considering risk-aversion is Choi and Ruszczyński (2008), where law invariant measures of risk[1] are used. The authors find structural properties of the optimal order quantity for an inventory problem without shortage penalty cost. Their work is extended in Choi et al. (2009) to the multi-product case.

The analysis of the inventory problem depends mainly on whether or not shortage penalty cost have to be considered. It can be seen that the presence of such shortage penalty cost might result in a major change in the optimal policy. As discussed earlier, shortage penalty cost is the per-unit cost of having too few units available, which exceeds the mere lost revenues, so $s = c_u - r > 0$. To understand the impact of penalty cost, we need to look at the relation between random demand and random profit, specifically at the correspondence between the ordered random demand and ordered profit in the sense that the n-lowest demand realization results in the n-lowest profit realization for each n.

Lemma 1. *Let D and Π be the random demand and profit, respectively, with realizations x and π. Without shortage penalty cost, so $s = 0$, there exists a one-to-one correspondence of the order of demand realizations x and the order of resulting profit realizations π.*

---

[1]Note that the concept of law invariant measures of risk is identical with spectral risk measures.

Proof. To show that without shortage penalty cost random profit has the same ordering as random demand, it is sufficient to see that in this case π is (weakly) monotone increasing in x. Using (1.5) we can write

$$\Pi(y,x) = \begin{cases} (p-c)x - (c-v)(y-x) & x \le y \\ (p-c)y & x > y. \end{cases} \qquad (3.1)$$

Hence, $\Pi(y,x)$ is increasing in x up to $x = y$ and then constant. □

A main consequence of Lemma 1 is that in the case $s = 0$, the operation becomes riskier the higher the order quantity is, and undesirable deviations from a certain profit level can always be reduced by ordering less initially (and hence accepting a lower expected profit). In the extreme case of not ordering at all, i. e. $y = 0$, both expected value and profit variability reduce to zero. However, once the decision maker considers shortage penalty cost, clearly this relation no longer holds. Minimizing risk now becomes a trade-off between costs resulting from overstocking and, unlike the previous case, costs from ordering too few due to shortage cost.

Hence, we will discuss the inventory problem with and without shortage penalty cost separately. In this chapter we will discuss the inventory problem with explicit consideration of risk preferences of the decision maker. While the focus is on the analysis under risk measures, in Section 3.1 we will start with a review of the existing literature on the problem, including approaches other than using risk measures, e. g. using the expected utility framework. Sections 3.2 and 3.3 are dedicated to the detailed analysis of the model with risk measures, without and with shortage penalty cost, respectively. Applications in the field of supply chain coordination and contracting under consideration of risk preferences will complete the chapter.

3.1 A review of inventory control with risk preferences

One of the early papers including risk aversion in the newsvendor context is Lau (1980), who considers three different objectives for a risk-averse newsvendor: a mean-deviation tradeoff, a utility function and the probability of achieving a minimum profit. Lau (1980) offers a formulation of the expected utility from profit with a utility function approximated by a polynomial. He gives an implicit solution for the optimal order quantity, but it can only be solved numerically and he cannot present properties of the optimal solution.

Eeckhoudt et al. (1995) examine the newsvendor problem with more general utility functions, but their setting is not the standard newsvendor setting: after demand realization, emergency ordering is possible at a cost of e where $c \leq e \leq p$. They show that risk aversion leads to lower order quantities.

Eeckhoudt et al. (1995) show:

1. If the newsvendor has decreasing absolute risk aversion, he orders more when he has larger initial wealth.

2. y^* increases in v and e similar to the risk-neutral case.

3. Changes in the cost and selling price can affect the order quantity in both directions. y^* might decrease as p increases and c decreases, which never happens in the risk-neutral case. The complication arises because of the two different effects of these parameters: the effect on the marginal benefit of y and the effect on the total wealth.

Wang et al. (2008) observed the last point shown by Eeckhoudt et al. (1995) in a numerical study and this observation caused a criticism of the expected utility theory for risk-averse newsvendor model. They observe that the newsvendor decreases his order quantity as the selling price increases, and in some cases it can be decreased almost to zero if the selling price is too high. A small degree of risk aversion for low to intermediate levels of return implies an irrationally high degree of risk aversion at the higher levels of return. While this problem was identified and treated in some fields of economics, "there is a lack of critical evaluation of expected utility theory for more complex settings such as the newsvendor problem" (Wang et al., 2008).

Keren and Pliskin (2006) solve the risk-averse newsvendor problem for a uniform demand distribution and provide a simple closed-form solution. They show that even with shortage penalty cost, a risk-averse newsvendor orders less than the risk-neutral. However, it is questionable how valuable the insights derived from using uniform distribution is since it might give counterintuitive results in case of risk aversion (see Collins, 2004).

Wang and Webster (2009) use a special form of utility functions: a piecewise linear loss aversion utility. The newsvendor considers his initial wealth as a reference level such that a final wealth below this level is considered as a loss and above it as a gain. He is more sensitive to losses than gains but within each region the utility is linear in wealth. They show that the risk aversion may lead to higher order quantities if the shortage cost is high and the relative uncertainty of demand is low.

Lau (1980) considers a mean-deviation objective with the standard deviation of profit as the deviation measure. When there is no shortage penalty, i. e. $s = 0$, he shows that the risk-averse newsvendor orders less than the risk-neutral one, and he claims that the same should hold when $s > 0$ without giving a proof because of the complexity of the problem. However, Wu et al. (2009) state that they disprove the claim of Lau (1980) for power distributed demand. They consider the case with positive shortage cost and they use the variance of profit as the deviation measure. They show that depending on the distribution parameter, the risk-averse newsvendor might order more than the risk-neutral. Chen and Federgruen (2000) come to the same result when they formulate the objective on cost parameters.

Chen and Federgruen (2000) model the risk-averse newsvendor problem in three different ways under the mean-variance criterion. One main result of the work is: for a risk-averse newsvendor, the two objectives, profit maximization and cost minimization, might result in different decisions. They explain this difference by the dependence of revenue and cost, which yields to: Var(Profit)$\neq$ Var(Revenue)+Var(Cost). Moreover, the decisions are different when the cost is formulated differently. They assume zero shortage cost and write the profit function for demand, D, as: $\Pi(y) = (p-c)y - (p-v)(y-D)^+$, and additionally they write two different cost functions which are equivalent when the newsvendor is risk-neutral: $C_1(y) = (c-v)(y-D)^+ + (p-c)(y-D)^-$ and $C_2(y) = -v(y-D)^+ + p(y-D)^- + cy$. When the mean-variance rule is applied for the profit, they show that the risk aversion leads to lower order quantities if $s = 0$. When the objective is defined as the minimization of expected cost and the variance of cost the result is more interesting. Assuming a power demand distribution as in Wu et al. (2009), they come up with the following result: depending on the distribution parameter, risk aversion may lead to higher order quantities even without shortage cost. Moreover, the size of overage and underage costs do not necessarily have an effect on this result. Hence, the difference between risk-averse and risk-neutral decision y^* is significantly affected by the specific demand distribution.

Collins (2004) shows similar results with numerical examples using the definition of overage cost c_o and underage cost c_u (recall the discussion in Section 1.1.1). He uses the mean-variance rule for the cost but he does not specify the cost parameters in detail. He uses c_o and c_u without decomposing them into shortage cost, salvage value, etc. For gamma, negative binomial, and normal demand distributions he shows that if the cost of underage is larger than the cost of overage, $c_u \geq c_o$, the risk-averse newsvendor orders more than the risk-neutral one. What defines the direction of the difference between the risk-averse and risk-neutral order quantity is the relative size of c_o and c_u, but not if they include shortage cost or not. Even if there are no shortage costs and no salvage value, if $c_u = p - c \geq c_o = c$, so the profit margin is more than 50%, the risk-averse newsvendor orders more than the risk-neutral one. However, such a result is not possible when the objective is written on profit.

When the mean-variance rule is applied on cost or profit, different results come up because of the variance factor. The means are optimized at the same level, which is the solution to the risk-neutral newsvendor. However, the variance of profit and the variance of cost shows different properties. When there is no shortage cost, the distribution of profit has a bound where demand equals order quantity. For all $D \geq y$ profit is the same, so the variance comes from the lower tail. In order to decrease this variance, the tail should be decreased which means decreasing order quantity. At the very extreme, when $y = 0$ there is no variance on profit. However, the distribution of cost has both tails even if $y = 0$. When the problem is formulated on cost it is written as $c_o = c - v$ and $c_u = p - c$, and each unit of demand above y costs c_u, which, in fact, is an opportunity cost. This term causes the distribution of cost to become unbounded. For each y the variance of cost is proportional to c_o, which comes from the lower tail of demand, and to c_u from the upper tail, and the quantity that gives the lowest variance depends on the relation of the two parameters, independent of their decomposition.

Collins (2004) points out an important issue: how critical it is to include risk aversion in the models. He mentions that in some cases the risk-averse and the risk-neutral solutions are so close that it might not be worth it to include risk aversion in the analysis and so to deal with complicated models. Specifically, for symmetrical demand distributions, if $c_o = c_u$ then the risk-averse and risk-neutral decisions are the same and the closer the two cost parameters are, the closer the solutions. Moreover, for the uniform distribution the two solutions are always equal independent of the difference between c_o and c_u. Since a uniform distribution is commonly used for numerical examples, this result is specifically important and one should be careful about deriving general insights from these examples.

As a third approach, Lau (1980) studied the problem of maximizing the probability of achieving a profit level L with and without shortage cost. When there is no shortage cost the result is quite simple: the optimal order quantity is $y^* = \frac{L}{p-c}$. Hence, the solution does not depend on the demand distribution at all, since the profit has a one-to-one correspondence with demand for all $D < y^*$, and for all $D \geq y^*$ it stays in the targeted level L. For any decrease in y^* it becomes impossible to reach L, and for any increase more demand is required to cover the cost c which means a decrease in the probability.

When the shortage cost is positive, given y, two different demand values can give the same profit level, so the distribution of profit is no longer a monotone function of demand. Lau (1980) presents the general solution method and gives explicit solutions for some demand distributions, such as normal and uniform distributions. Interestingly, for the uniform distribution, the optimal order quantity does not depend on salvage value at all.

From the discussion on mean-deviation objective, we know that when the problem is formulated in terms of cost, the solution becomes more complicated. Independent of shortage cost, the monotonic behaviour in demand ceases to exist and we expect that a simple solution like the one presented by Lau (1980) cannot be valid anymore.

After the axiomatic foundation of coherent risk measures by Artzner et al. (1999), the application of risk measures in inventory modeling became popular. CVaR_α, specifically, has become an important measure of risk in inventory modeling. Jammernegg and Kischka (2007) study the CVaR_α problem focusing on the effect of risk aversion on performance measures. They formulate the objective function as a convex combination of the expected profit and the CVaR_α of profit, so that they can cover both risk-averse and risk-seeking behaviour. Ahmed et al. (2007) solve the CVaR maximization problem for the newsvendor model with shortage cost. They formulate the objective in terms of cost, and the focus is on proving the existence of an optimal solution. Inclusion of shortage cost and the different formulation does not allow a simple solution, but they show that an optimum exists. Gotoh and Takano (2007) consider both the CVaR_α and mean-CVaR_α models with shortage cost. They use two different objectives, one formulated on profit and one on cost. In the following sections, the CVaR_α and mean-CVaR_α models are analyzed in more detail.

3.2 Basic inventory control problem

In the following section we will analyze the newsvendor's inventory problem under spectral risk measures and derive the optimality conditions. We will derive some structural properties about the optimal solution, i. e. the optimal order quantity. Further, we discuss the problem with respect to different performance measures such as the cycle service level. After having discussed the inventory problem with general risk spectra, we will look at special cases of risk spectra such as the $CVaR_\alpha$ or mean-$CVaR_\alpha$ formulations as well as some continuous risk spectra such as the power and exponential function, in Section 3.2.2. We will conclude this section with a numerical analysis of the inventory problem for different formulations of the demand distribution and risk spectrum.

3.2.1 Optimal policy and structural properties for the basic inventory problem

We are now ready to apply general risk spectra to the basic inventory control problem, i. e. the newsvendor problem without shortage penalty cost.

Proposition 4 (Newsvendor with a general risk measure). *Let the objective function of a newsvendor using a spectral risk measure be*

$$\max_{y \in \mathbb{R}^+} M(\Pi(y)), \tag{3.2}$$

where

$$M(\Pi(y)) = (p - c)y - (p - v) \int_0^y (y - x)\phi(F(x))f(x)\, dx. \tag{3.3}$$

The risk measure is concave in the order quantity y, and the optimal order quantity y^*, is

$$y^* = F^{-1}\left(\Phi^{-1}\left(\frac{p - c}{p - v}\right)\right), \tag{3.4}$$

where $\Phi^{-1}(\omega)$ denotes the inverse risk transformation function.

See Appendix A for a proof.

This result shows us that the optimal order quantity of a newsvendor optimizing a measure using a general risk spectrum can be expressed in a very compact way. While for a risk-neutral newsvendor the critical fractile $\frac{p-c}{p-v}$ refers directly to the optimal cycle service level, CSL^*, a risk-averse or risk-seeking newsvendor will deviate from this solution.

Based on Proposition 4 we can obtain structural properties of the optimal solution with respect to the cost parameters as with the risk-neutral problem. From the monotonicity of F and Φ we can immediately derive the following

Corollary 3. *The optimal cycle service level CSL^* and the optimal order quantity y^* are increasing in the selling price p and salvage value v and decreasing in cost c.*

Note that these results are in line with the results for the risk-neutral newsvendor. In the following proposition we derive structural results about the optimal cycle service level and the optimal order quantity with respect to the risk preference using (3.4).

Proposition 5. *For a newsvendor without shortage penalty cost, the optimal cycle service level CSL^* and the order quantity y^* increase in the risk preference η.*

Proof. From Definition 6 we know that Φ decreases in η, and its inverse Φ^{-1} increases in η. It follows immediately that y^* increases in η. □

This result generalizes results previously described in the literature. For a newsvendor applying a $CVaR_\alpha$ objective function, Chen et al. (2004) show that the optimal order quantity for a risk-averse newsvendor will not exceed the risk-neutral optimal order quantity. For different formulations of mean-deviation rules similar results were found. Jammernegg and Kischka (2007) find that the optimal order quantity is increasing in α (i.e. decreasing in the level of risk aversion) and decreasing in λ (higher values of λ puts higher weights on the α-quantile and lower weights on the expected value and, hence, imply a higher level of risk aversion).

The intuition behind this behaviour is clear: Since the newsvendor incurs no shortage penalty cost other than lost profit $p - c$, the risk in profit comes only from unsold leftover inventory. Hence, by reducing the order quantity, the newsvendor can always reduce his risk by accepting the reduced expected profit. Later in Section 3.3 we will see that in the case of positive shortage penalty cost this is no longer true.

Continuing the discussion about non-strict ordering of Φ from Section 2.3.1, where we gave an example of two intersecting risk transformation functions in Figure 3.1, we can see now that in this case the order of the optimal cycle service level and order quantity depends on the critical fractile. For smaller ranges of the target cycle service level, decision maker DM_1 will order more than decision maker DM_2 and act less risk-averse; for larger ranges this relation will change. While for some ranges of the critical fractile, e.g. for low selling prices, decision maker DM_1 orders more than DM_2, but as the critical fractile increases this relation changes.

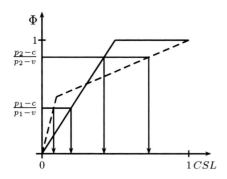

Figure 3.1: Two decision makers with different risk spectra: DM_1 with CVaR_α risk spectrum, $\alpha = 0.5$ (solid line), DM_2 with mean-CVaR_α risk spectrum, $\alpha = 0.1$, $\lambda = 0.5$ (dashed line). Note that the optimal cycle service level is the transformed critical fractile. For a low price p_1 DM_1 orders more than DM_2, while for a high price p_2 this relation changes.

Proposition 6. *The expected profit $\mathbb{E}\,\Pi$ of a newsvendor using a spectral measure of risk is maximized for the risk-neutral optimal order quantity. $\mathbb{E}\,\Pi$ decreases the more the newsvendor's risk preference deviates from risk neutrality.*

Proof. Recall that $\mathbb{E}\,\Pi$ is concave in y, with its maximum in the risk-neutral optimal order quantity. From Proposition 5 we know that y^* increases in η. Hence, $\mathbb{E}\,\Pi$ is unimodal in the risk preference. $\qquad\qquad\square$

This result was already described by Jammernegg and Kischka (2007) for a newsvendor using a mean-CVaR_α risk spectrum (see the discussion later in Example 6).

While the cycle service level can be seen as an external, i.e. customer oriented performance measure, the probability of missing a profit target level as defined in (1.9) is an internally oriented performance measure.

Lemma 2. *Let L be a given profit target level. The probability of missing the profit level L is the probability that profit is below the target. For a newsvendor without shortage penalty cost*

$$PL_L := \mathbb{P}(\Pi \leq L) = \begin{cases} F\left(\frac{(c-v)y+L}{p-v}\right) & \text{for } L \leq (p-c)y \\ 1 & \text{for } L > (p-c)y. \end{cases} \qquad (3.5)$$

Hence, in the case of $y \geq \frac{L}{p-c}$, PL_L is monotone increasing in y.

See Appendix A for a proof.

Note that in the special case $L = 0$ the probability of any negative profit realization is considered (cf. Jammernegg and Kischka, 2007).

Proposition 7. *Let a newsvendor with a general admissible risk spectrum order y^* such that it maximizes his risk measure $\mathrm{M}(y)$. PL_L increases in the risk preference for any $L \leq (p-c)y$ and is 1 otherwise.*

Proof. Using Proposition 5, the optimal order quantity y^* increases in η. From Lemma 2, PL_L increases in y for $L \leq (p-c)y$ and is 1 otherwise. Hence, PL_L increases in the risk preference for $L \leq (p-c)y$ and is 1 otherwise. □

This result was already found by Jammernegg and Kischka (2007) for a mean-CVaR$_\alpha$ decision maker for the case $L = 0$. In this case the optimal probability of missing the profit target is increasing in α and decreasing in λ. Very related to Proposition 7 is Lau (1980), who describes a situation where a budgeted profit might be established such that a manager may be interested primarily in maximizing the probability of reaching this budget. In this case it might be less important if the limit is strongly exceeded or just reached. Lau (1980) derives the optimal order quantity which we can formulate in the following:

Corollary 4 (Maximizing the probability of reaching a profit target). *The optimal order quantity y^*, which maximizes the probability of reaching a certain profit target level L, is*

$$y^* = \frac{L}{p-c} \qquad (3.6)$$

On this result Lau (1980) comments "This result is somewhat strange: to maximize the probability of attaining L, one sets the decision variable such that L is also the largest possible profit attainable." However, we think this result is quite intuitive: since the profit distributions are ordered with respect to y up to $(p-c)y$, once the newsvendor already ordered $y^* = \frac{L}{p-c}$ there is no benefit from ordering a single unit more, since the maximum potential profit increase is not considered, while the worst profit outcome, $-cy$, is decreasing. If the newsvendor orders one unit less than (3.6), he cannot reach the profit target level at all.

Let us state here that the primary use in this work of the probability of missing a profit target level is as performance measure, not as objective function. Hence, the result of Corollary 4 is mainly presented for the sake of completeness. Among the recent works, Shi and Chen (2007) consider maximizing the probability of reaching a profit target level in a supply chain context, and in Shi et al. (2010) a combined inventory and pricing approach is taken.

3.2.2 Specific examples of risk spectra in the basic inventory problem

Using some examples, we will now show how the general spectral measure can be used to solve the inventory problem for already-known formulations, such as the expected value solution, the $CVaR_\alpha$ objective function or a mean-deviation objective where deviation is expressed by $CVaR_\alpha$. As all of these formulations are special cases of spectral measures, the examples illustrate the flexibility of using general risk spectra in the problem analysis.

Example 4 (Expected value). A first example is the expected value formulation derived in (1.4). Using the expected value implies neutrality about the variability of the outcome, hence the spectral function does not assess higher weights to lower outcomes. The risk spectrum is

$$\phi(\omega) = 1. \tag{3.7}$$

It can be easily seen that applying (3.7) to (3.4) results in the optimal order quantity for a risk-neutral newsvendor

$$y^* = F^{-1}\left(\frac{p-c}{p-v}\right)$$

as previously stated in (1.4).

Example 5 ($CVaR_\alpha$). As we discussed earlier in Section 2.3 when describing the general spectral measure, $CVaR_\alpha$ is another special case where the risk spectrum is a constant function $\frac{1}{\alpha}$ in the range $0\ldots\alpha$ as in (2.10), so that the risk transformation function is

$$\Phi(\omega) = \begin{cases} \omega\frac{1}{\alpha} & \omega \leq \alpha \\ 1 & \text{otherwise.} \end{cases} \tag{3.8}$$

Its inverse is then

$$\Phi^{-1}(t) = \alpha t \qquad \text{for } t \in [0,1] \tag{3.9}$$

so that the optimal order quantity is

$$y^* = F^{-1}\left(\alpha \cdot \frac{p-c}{p-v}\right). \tag{3.10}$$

This result can be found for example in an early draft of Chen et al. (2004), who, in their work, specifically used the CVaR_α objective function to model risk-averse decision making behaviour.

An observation we can make for a CVaR_α spectrum is that the optimal cycle service level is limited by α. If we consider DM_1 in Figure 3.1 again (the solid line), then it is easy to see that the maximum cycle service level $CSL_{\text{max}} = \alpha$ is reached for $\Phi = 1$, so for $\lim_{p \to \infty} \frac{p-c}{p-v}$. This implies that independent of the profitability of the product, the optimal order quantity will not exceed a certain amount, $F^{-1}(\alpha)$.

This implies, for the distribution of profit, that the optimal order quantity will be such that $\text{VaR}_\alpha(\Pi(y^*)) = (p - c)y^*$ (see Gotoh and Takano, 2007, or Chen et al., 2008b). The intuition behind this is that a CVaR_α decision maker only considers profit outcomes below VaR_α; any realization above VaR_α is not considered. Hence, using the fact that the maximum possible profit realization under the "best" demand state is $(p-c)y$, there is no benefit from ordering any quantity where the resulting $\text{VaR}_\alpha(\Pi(y))$ is smaller than $(p - c)y$.

Example 6 (Mean-CVaR_α objective). The mean-CVaR_α objective function is a special case where the risk spectrum is a piecewise constant function with a single step in α as in (2.11). Recall that this risk spectrum has two paramters. It is composed out of a CVaR_α part with parameter α and the expected value in a convex combination, where the weighting factor is λ. Its risk transformation function is

$$\Phi(\omega) = \begin{cases} \frac{\lambda}{\alpha}\omega & \omega \le \alpha \\ \lambda + \frac{1-\lambda}{1-\alpha}(\omega - \alpha) & \text{otherwise.} \end{cases} \tag{3.11}$$

The inverse risk transformation function in this case is

$$\Phi^{-1}(t) = \begin{cases} \frac{\alpha}{\lambda}t & t \le \lambda \\ \alpha + \frac{1-\alpha}{1-\lambda}(t - \lambda) & \text{otherwise.} \end{cases} \tag{3.12}$$

Plugging (3.12) in (3.4) leads to the optimal order quantity

$$y^* = \begin{cases} F^{-1}\left(\frac{\alpha}{\lambda}\frac{p-c}{p-v}\right) & \frac{p-c}{p-v} \le \lambda \\ F^{-1}\left(\frac{p-c}{p-v} + \frac{\alpha-\lambda}{1-\lambda}\frac{c-v}{p-v}\right) & \text{otherwise.} \end{cases} \tag{3.13}$$

A mean-CVaR_α objective of this type was already proposed and the optimal policy found in Jammernegg and Kischka (2007) and Gotoh and Takano

(2007). While the latter are mainly interested in finding a linear programming formulation for solving the capacity constraint multi-product case, Jammernegg and Kischka (2007) derive structural properties for the risk-averse ($\alpha < \lambda$) as well as for the risk-seeking ($\alpha > \lambda$) behaviour. They show that the optimal order quantity y^* and the optimal cycle service level CSL are increasing in α and decreasing in λ, hence decreasing in the level of risk aversion.

Note that as long as the critical fractile $\frac{p-c}{p-v}$ is smaller than λ, the solution of the mean-CVaR$_\alpha$ optimizer is not different from the pure CVaR$_\alpha$ optimizer.

Further, Jammernegg and Kischka (2007) point out that expected profit decreases the more risk-averse or risk-seeking the decision maker becomes. This result can be obtained considering the fact that the optimal order quantity of a risk-neutral decision maker results in the maximum expected profit, and by the monotonicity of the order quantity in the risk preference.

3.2.3 Numerical study of the basic inventory control problem

In this section we will present a numerical study in order to illustrate the findings introduced in the previous section and will discuss some of the structural properties of the problem in more detail.

For numerical analysis of the basic inventory control problem we use the following parameters: selling price $p = 10$, production cost $c = 6$, salvage value $v = 3$, no shortage penalty costs are considered (see Section 3.3.3 for numerics of the inventory problem with positive shortage penalty cost). Additionally, for the mean-CVaR$_\alpha$ risk spectrum, whenever it is not stated otherwise, we set $\lambda = 0.5$.

To model demand uncertainty, in the following we assume two parametric distributions of demand.

1. A *Weibull* distribution $D \sim \text{Weib}(2, 100)$ is used as a general rule, since it is shown to be a "Newsvendor distribution" by Braden and Freimer (1991). The expected demand, $\mathbb{E}\,D = 88.62$ units, the optimal risk-neutral cycle service level is $CSL^* = 0.5714$ and the corresponding optimal order quantity is $y^* = F^{-1}(0.5714) = 92.05$ units.

2. A *Gamma* distribution $D \sim \text{Gamma}(\mu, \sigma^2)$ will be used for all cases where the effect of demand variance is of interest, since the Gamma distribution allows for changing variance while keeping the mean constant, which is not possible for the Weibull distribution. Expected

demand is again $\mathbb{E}\,D = \mu = 88.62$; CSL^* and y^* depend on the actual variance.

Note that both distributions have a positive support which fits with the assumption of a non-negative demand D, unlike the commonly used normal distribution.

We use the following definitions of both distribution functions. We define the Weibull distribution with two parameters, the shape γ and scale δ parameter, as

$$F(x) = 1 - e^{-\left(\frac{x}{\delta}\right)^{\gamma}}, \tag{3.14}$$

with corresponding density,

$$f(x) = \frac{\gamma}{\delta}\left(\frac{x}{\delta}\right)^{\gamma-1} e^{-\left(\frac{x}{\delta}\right)^{\gamma}}. \tag{3.15}$$

For the Gamma distribution we use as parameters mean μ and variance σ^2 directly, so that we can modify them independently. Hence, we define the cdf as

$$F(x) = \frac{\gamma\left(\frac{\mu^2}{\sigma}, x\frac{\mu}{\sigma}\right)}{\Gamma\left(\frac{\mu^2}{\sigma}\right)}, \tag{3.16}$$

where here Γ is defined as the complete Gamma function and γ is the lower incomplete Gamma function[2]. All numerics are calculated using the R language and environment for statistical computing (R Development Core Team, 2010).

Results from the numerical study

As stated in Proposition 5, y^* is monotone in the level of risk aversion for the inventory problem without shortage penalty cost. Figure 3.2 shows the monotonicity of y^* in the level of risk aversion for a mean-CVaR$_\alpha$ and a power risk spectrum. Note that in the mean-CVaR$_\alpha$ model, for a fixed α, y^* is decreasing in λ, which can be seen from the perfect ordering of the y^* lines in the first plot of Figure 3.2.

---

[2]The Gamma function is defined as $\Gamma(z) := \int_0^\infty t^{z-1}e^{-t}\,dt$. The lower incomplete gamma function is defined on the same integrand, $\gamma(z,r) := \int_0^r t^{z-1}e^{-t}\,dt$. Note that there exist efficient numerical approximations for the (incomplete) Gamma function as well as for the probability and density of the Gamma distribution in the R environment for statistical computing.

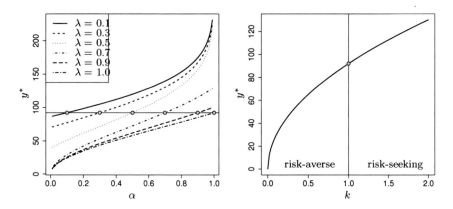

Figure 3.2: Optimal order quantity y^* for a mean-CVaR$_\alpha$ (left plot) and a power (right plot) risk spectrum objective function. Note that the circles on the lines correspond to the risk-neutral y^* and for each line separate between risk-averse (left) and risk-seeking (right) behaviour.

In Figure 3.2 we can see that the risk preference can have a big impact on y^*. For example, with the power risk spectrum, y^* changes between 20 and 120. However, the size of the difference depends on the parameters of the demand distribution. Figure 3.3 shows the effect of demand variance on y^*. The lines are ordered with respect to η and they get more and more distant as variance increases. Clearly, risk preference is an issue of uncertainty or randomness, and if we see variance as a measure of uncertainty, it is obvious that large variance causes a more significant impact of the risk preference on the decision.

In Figure 3.4 we illustrate the expected profit evaluated at y^* with respect to the risk preference obtained by maximizing the risk-measure for a mean-CVaR$_\alpha$ and a power risk spectrum. Clearly, the expected profit is maximized in the risk-neutral case and decreases when the decision maker deviates from risk neutrality, becoming more risk-averse or more risk-seeking. Hence, there are some profit levels smaller than the risk-neutral expected profit which can be reached by an order quantity which is optimal for a specific risk-averse, as well as for a risk-seeking, decision maker.

Figure 3.5 considers a 90% confidence interval of profit, CI Π, and the maximum and minimum possible profits, $\pi_{\max}$ and $\pi_{\min}$, respectively. For most of the α-levels and all k the upper border of the confidence interval

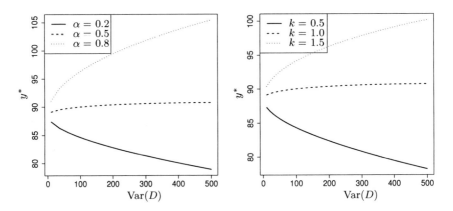

Figure 3.3: Optimal order quantity y^* for a mean-CVaR_α (left) and power (right) risk spectrum as a function of demand variance σ^2, where $D \sim \mathrm{Gamma}(\mu, \sigma^2)$.

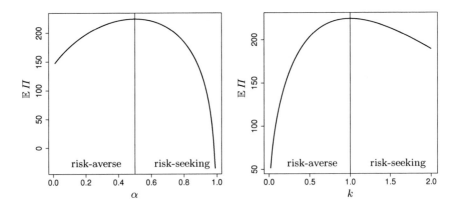

Figure 3.4: Expected profit with corresponding y^* for a mean-CVaR_α (left plot) and a power (right plot) risk spectrum with demand $D \sim \mathrm{Weib}(2,100)$. Note that the vertical line separates risk-averse ($\alpha < \lambda$ and $k < 1$) from risk-seeking ($\alpha > \lambda$ and $k > 1$) behaviour.

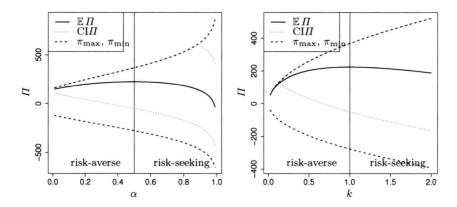

Figure 3.5: Expected profit with corresponding y^* for a mean-CVaR$_\alpha$ (left plot) and a power (right plot) risk spectrum with a 90% confidence interval CI Π and maximum/minimum profit π_{max} and π_{min}, respectively.

corresponds to π_{max}. Note that the size of the confidence interval, as well as the range $\pi_{max} - \pi_{min}$, is increasing in η.

In Figure 3.6 the probability of missing different profit targets is shown. As the left plot shows, PL_L is 1 for order quantities below $(p - c)y$ and increasing in y for any quantity larger than this threshold. It can be easily seen that PL_L is ordered with respect to the target level L in the sense that the higher the profit target level, the larger PL_L is. The right plot shows PL_L at y^* with respect to the level of risk aversion, specifically with respect to k for a power risk spectrum. The structure shown in the left plot is almost directly carried on to the right one because of the monotonicity of y^* in k.

3.3 Inventory control with shortage penalty cost

We will now discuss the case where the newsvendor considers shortage penalty cost in addition to lost revenues in case of a stockout situation for each unit short. Similar to the basic inventory problem without shortage cost we will formulate the problem for a general risk spectrum and illustrate properties for specific examples afterwards.

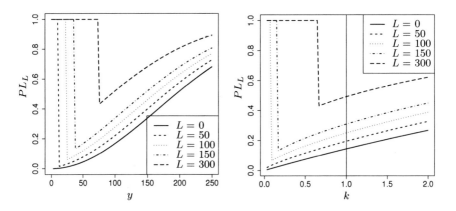

Figure 3.6: Probability of missing a profit target L, i.e. $\mathbb{P}(\Pi \leq L)$ with different order quantities (left) and with the degree of risk aversion k, where the corresponding optimal order quantity for a power risk spectrum is used.

3.3.1 Optimal policy and structural properties for the inventory problem with shortage penalty costs

Once the newsvendor considers shortage penalty cost for unsatisfied demand, the ordering of profit is not the same as of demand anymore, as discussed in Lemma 1. If we consider for now the maximum possible profit realization for a given quantity y as the profit target, so $\Pi_L = (p - c)y$, then a deviation of this profit target can happen now for a demand realization larger than y (i.e. profit loss due to understocking) in addition to the realizations smaller than y (i.e. profit loss due to overstocking).

Recall that the newsvendor's profit function with shortage penalty cost can be written as

$$\Pi(y) = \begin{cases} (p - c)D - (c - v)(y - D) & D \leq y \\ (p - c)y - s(D - y) & D > y, \end{cases} \tag{3.17}$$

with cdf $F_\Pi(\pi) = \mathbb{P}(\Pi(y) \leq \pi)$.

In Figure 3.7 the profit distribution for a newsvendor without and with shortage penalty cost are shown. The cdf of profit without shortage penalty cost has a jump in $(p - c)y$ to 1, since there is a probability mass on this profit realization. For the case with shortage penalty cost such a point does not exist, and therefore the profit cdf is continuous. Further, without shortage penalty cost, the minimum possible profit is $-(c - v)y$ and the profit

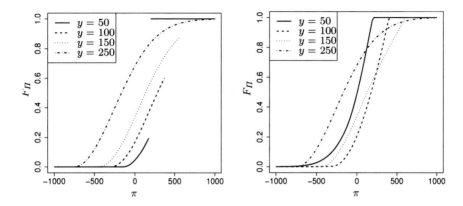

Figure 3.7: Cumulative distribution function of profit without considering (left), and while considering (right) shortage penalty cost with parameters $p = 10$, $c = 6$, $v = 3$; $s = 0$ (left) and $s = 5$ (right).

distribution has a limited support to the left. With shortage penalty cost the minimum possible profit is $-\infty$ with demand ∞, so the profit distribution has unlimited support on the left tail.

Figure 3.8 depicts profit with respect to demand for a given quantity, y. Note that the maximum possible profit is $\pi_{\max} = (p - c)y$. Let us for now consider any profit $\pi_1 \in [-(c - v)y, (p - c)y)$. Each profit in this range will happen with exactly two different demand realizations; with demand $x_1 < y$ and with a corresponding demand $\bar{x}_1 > y$. Equating both cases of (3.17) for $\pi(x, y)$, we can express $\bar{x}$ in terms of x, so

$$\bar{x} = y + (y - x)\frac{p - v}{s}. \tag{3.18}$$

Note that the corresponding upper demand level $\bar{x}$ for a given x depends on y. This becomes immediately clear from Figure 3.8 if we keep x constant and increase y. In this case $\pi_{\max}$ increases. Since the slopes of both parts of this piecewise linear function stay the same ($p - v$ for $x \leq y$ and $-s$ for $x > y$), $\bar{x}$ is necessarily increasing.

From Figure 3.8 we can see that the probability that profit is below π_1 is composed of two parts: (a) the probability that demand is below x, and (b) the probability that demand is larger than $\bar{x}$. From (3.18) we can express $\bar{x}$ as a function of x, so we are able to express the sum of the

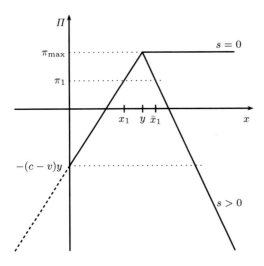

Figure 3.8: Profit Π as a function of random demand D. Maximum profit π_{max} is reached for $D = y$. If no shortage penalty cost are considered ($s = 0$), Π remains constant for any $D > y$, while for the case with shortage penalty cost ($s > 0$), Π decreases in D. Note that in the latter case, each profit realization above $-(c - v)y$ can happen with exactly two different demand levels.

two probabilities in terms of $x < y$ as long as we also consider negative realizations of demand. Profit realizations below $-(c - v)y$ can only occur in the case where demand $D > y\left(1 + \frac{p-v}{s}\right)$, which would correspond to $x < 0$. Hence, if we only consider the demands in the range $(-\infty, y]$ or alternatively, $[y, \infty)$, we are able to cover all possible profit realizations. In the following analysis we will use the range $(-\infty, y]$, which implies considering negative demand realizations $x < 0$, although they happen with probability 0.

Lemma 3 (Profit distribution). *Let Π be random profit with distribution $F_\Pi(\pi)$ and D random demand with distribution $F(x)$. There exist two mutually exclusive demand levels, $x \in (-\infty, y]$ and $\bar{x} \in (y, \infty)$ where profit equals π. Hence,*

$$F_\Pi(\pi) = \begin{cases} F\left(\frac{\pi + (c-v)y}{p-v}\right) + 1 - F\left(\frac{(p-c+s)y - \pi}{s}\right) & \text{for } \pi \leq (p-c)y \\ 1 & \text{for } \pi > (p-c)y, \end{cases} \quad (3.19)$$

with density

$$f_\Pi(\pi) = \begin{cases} \frac{1}{p-v} f\left(\frac{\pi + (c-v)y}{p-v}\right) + \frac{1}{s} f\left(\frac{(p-c+s)y - \pi}{s}\right) & \text{for } \pi \leq (p-c)y \\ 0 & \text{for } \pi > (p-c)y. \end{cases}$$

$$(3.20)$$

See Appendix A for a proof. Since we formulated the profit distribution for $x < y$ in Lemma 3, by (3.17) x is such that $\pi(x, y) = (p - c)x - (c - v)(y - x)$. Plugging in $\pi(x, y)$ in (3.19),

$$F_\Pi\Big(\pi(x, y)\Big) = F(x) + 1 - F\left(y + (y - x)\frac{p - v}{s}\right).$$

Further, since we previously defined $\bar{x} := y + (y - x)\frac{p-v}{s}$,

$$F_\Pi\Big(\pi(x, y)\Big) = F(x) + 1 - F(\bar{x}). \tag{3.21}$$

Note that (3.21) forms a new distribution function for any $x \le y$. Considering (3.18), in the following we call the new distribution function $G(x) := F_\Pi\Big(\pi(x, y)\Big) = F(x) + 1 - F(\bar{x})$ with density $g(x) := f(x) + f(\bar{x})\frac{p-v}{s}$. Note that even if we do not write it explicitly, the order quantity y is a parameter of the distribution function $G(x)$.

In light of the above discussion we are now ready to formulate the risk measure in the following proposition.

Proposition 8 (Newsvendor with a general risk measure). *Let the objective function of a newsvendor using a spectral risk measure be*

$$\max_{y \in \mathbb{R}^+} \mathrm{M}(\Pi(y)), \tag{3.22}$$

where

$$\mathrm{M}(\Pi(y)) := (p - c)y - (p - v) \int_{-\infty}^{y} G_\phi(x)\, dx \tag{3.23}$$

and

$$G_\phi(x) := \Phi(G(x)) = \Phi\Big(F(x) + 1 - F(\bar{x})\Big).$$

The risk measure is concave in the order quantity y. Furthermore, we can write the optimal order quantity y^* as the solution to the first order condition,

$$\mathrm{M}'(\Pi(y^*)) = \frac{d\,\mathrm{M}(\Pi(y))}{dy}\bigg|_{y=y^*} = 0, \tag{3.24}$$

*where the first derivative of the risk measure with respect to the order quantity
y is*

$$
\begin{aligned}
\mathrm{M}'(y) = & \int_{-\infty}^{y} (-(c-v)g(x)\phi\Big(G(x)\Big)\,dx \\
& + \int_{-\infty}^{y} \pi(x,y)\frac{dg(x)}{dy}\phi\Big(G(x)\Big)\,dx \\
& + \int_{-\infty}^{y} \pi(x,y)g(x)^2\phi'\Big(G(x)\Big)\,dx \\
& + (p-c)yf(y)\phi(1)\left(1+\frac{p-v}{s}\right).
\end{aligned}
\tag{3.25}
$$

See Appendix A for a proof.

The concavity result follows from the general results obtained by Acerbi
(2002) stated in Proposition 3(a). As mentioned earlier, $G(x)$ forms a new
distribution function on demand for a specific order quantity, so that for each
y a different G exists. For a given y, one can think of G as cdf of the sum of
two exclusive, conditional random demands. Hence, when shortage penalty
costs are considered, we can transform the demand distribution F into a
distribution G such that the same ordering of profit and demand exists.
Important, however, is that now we have to consider negative demand
realizations. Although having a probability of zero, each of them has a
corresponding positive demand realization $x > y$, where the newsvendor
incurs shortage penalty costs.

Instead of explicitly formulating $\mathrm{M}(\Pi)$ for the case of a risk-averse decision
maker, one could also use the maximization formula by Acerbi (2002) directly.
However, to be able to solve (2.15) numerically, the risk spectrum has to
be discretized into a piecewise linear function with a resolution of J steps.
This discretized ϕ can be used for an optimization using (2.18). However,
the complexity of the optimization problem grows in the number of steps
since the optimization has to be carried out over (y, ψ^J), or $J+1$ variables.
Additionally, for the case of a risk-seeking decision maker a joint optimization
on (y, ψ) does not seem possible anyway.

Using (3.23) together with (3.25) allows for using highly efficient single
dimensional numerical optimization algorithms. The reason why we are
able to reduce the $(J+1)$-dimensional optimization problem to a single
dimensional one is that we are taking advantage of the specific ordering of
profit realizations, while Acerbi's method does not assume any knowledge

on the ordering of profit[3]. A more detailed discussion about the derivation can be found in the proof of Proposition 8 in Appendix A.

3.3.2 Specific examples of risk spectra in the inventory problem with shortage penalty cost

As we did in the previous section for the basic inventory control problem, we can now look at special cases of risk spectra already used in the literature and describe the optimal policies and structural properties found so far. Note again, that for the risk-neutral case, i. e. for the expected value optimization, $\phi(\omega) = 1$, the transformations described in the previous section are not necessary. When all random realizations are given the same weight, the different ordering of the demand realizations compared to profit realizations is not relevant. It is easy to find the optimal order quantity y^* for this case as $y^* = F^{-1}\left(\frac{p-c+s}{p-v+s}\right)$; see the discussion of the risk-neutral problem in the introduction in Section 1.1.1. In the following, we will give as examples the pure CVaR_α optimizer and a mean-CVaR_α optimizer.

Example 7 (CVaR_α decision maker with shortage penalty cost). Unlike the general formulation of the optimal order quantity in 3.25 the problem can be solved for the optimal order quantity y^* in closed form in the following

Lemma 4 (Optimal order quantity for a CVaR_α optimizer with shortage penalty cost).

$$y^* = \frac{p-v}{p-v+s}F^{-1}\left(\alpha\frac{p-c+s}{p-v+s}\right) + \frac{s}{p-v+s}F^{-1}\left(1 - \alpha\frac{c-v}{p-v+s}\right). \tag{3.26}$$

See Appendix A for a proof.

While this explicit formulation specifically for the CVaR_α decision maker of the optimal policy was previously derived by Gotoh and Takano (2007), we present a proof based on the optimization of (3.22). Their original proof is based on the CVaR_α optimization by Rockafellar and Uryasev (2000) and solves the problem for both y^* and optimal Value-at-Risk ψ^*. Note that the case without shortage penalty cost is a special case of (3.26); as for $s = 0$, the right term vanishes and the weighting factor for the first term becomes 1, so that the whole equation reduces to the solution of the CVaR_α solution without shortage penalty cost in (3.10).

---

[3]Note that Acerbi (2002) calls the problem of not knowing the ordering of profit with respect to the state variable "reshuffling" of profit.

Example 8 (Mean-CVaR$_\alpha$ decision maker with shortage penalty cost).
Extending the results of the CVaR$_\alpha$ decision maker of the previous example
leads to the result of a mean-CVaR$_\alpha$ decision maker.

Lemma 5 (Optimal order quantity for a mean-CVaR$_\alpha$ optimizer with
shortage penalty cost). *The optimal order quantity y^* is that y which solves
the following system of equations*

$$\frac{\lambda}{\alpha}\Big((p-c+s)(1-F(\bar{x}^o))-(c-v)F(x^o)\Big)$$

$$+\frac{1-\lambda}{1-\alpha}\Big((p-c+s)F(\bar{x}^o)+(c-v)F(x^o)-(p-v+s)F(y)\Big)=0 \quad (3.27)$$

$$F(x^o)+1-F(\bar{x}^o)=\alpha. \quad (3.28)$$

The proof is omitted here and provided with Example 9 where a general
piecewise constant risk spectrum is considered.

It seems to be impossible to find an explicit formulation for y^* for general
demand distributions, although for specific families of distributions an explicit
solution can be obtained by plugging in the distribution function. Solving
both equations numerically is highly efficient compared to applying numerical
optimization algorithms on $M(\Pi(y))$ as defined in (3.23) directly, since no
numerical integration has to be carried out.[4]

Example 9 (General piecewise constant risk spectrum with shortage penalty
cost). The results of the mean-CVaR$_\alpha$ example can be further generalized
by considering a piecewise constant risk spectrum, e.g. to discretize a
continuous risk spectrum in a piecewise constant function with J jumps as
shown and discussed in Section 2.3.3. The risk spectrum in ω was already
shown in Figure 2.5, while the corresponding inventory problem is illustrated
in Figure 3.9. If J jumps exist, then there are $J+1$ levels of ϕ, so $\phi_1 \ldots \phi_{J+1}$.
The demands where the jumps occur are then $x_1 \ldots x_J$. Further, we define
$x_0^o := -\infty$ and $x_{J+1}^o := y$, i.e. the smallest and largest demand realization
in the demand range of interest. Recall from the discussion in Section 3.3.1
that considering the demand range $(-\infty, y]$ is enough to cover all possible
profit realizations.

---

[4]The computation of the distribution function might require numerical integration
   techniques, if no closed-form expression exists. An example for such a cdf is the
   Gamma distribution. In those cases, generally efficient approximations implemented
   in numerical software packages (e.g. R) exist.

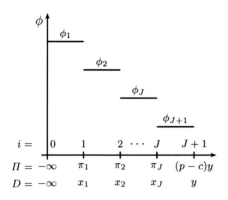

Figure 3.9: A discretized risk spectrum with J jumps in the probability range, so that $J + 1$ levels of ϕ exist. The profit levels at the borders of each range i are $\Pi_i = -\infty, \pi_1, \ldots, \pi_J, (p - c)y$, with corresponding demand levels below y of $D = -\infty, x_1^o, \ldots, x_J^o, y$.

Lemma 6 (Optimal order quantity of a newsvendor with piecewise constant risk spectrum considering shortage penalty cost). *Let x_i^o be the demand where*

$$F(x_i^o) + 1 - F(\bar{x}_i^o) = \omega_i, \qquad (3.29)$$

so that x_i^o are the demands in the range $(-\infty, y]$ up to which point the profits are weighted with ϕ_i. We can formulate M *using a piecewise constant ϕ as*

$$\mathrm{M}(\Pi(y)) = \sum_{i=1}^{J+1} \phi_i \int_{x_{i-1}^o}^{x_i^o} \Big((p - c)x - (c - v)(y - x) \Big) g(x)\, dx. \qquad (3.30)$$

The optimal order quantity y^* satisfies the following system of equations (i. e. the first order condition):

$$\frac{d\,\mathrm{M}(\Pi(y))}{dy} = 0 =$$

$$= \sum_{i=1}^{J+1} \phi_i \Big((p - c + s)(F(\bar{x}_{i-1}^o) - F(\bar{x}_i^o)) - (c - v)(F(x_i^o) - F(x_{i-1}^o)) \Big),$$

$$\qquad (3.31)$$

$$F(x_i^o) + 1 - F(\bar{x}_i^o) = \omega_i \quad \text{for all } i = 1 \ldots J. \qquad (3.32)$$

See Appendix A for a proof.

Note that for J jumps a system of $J + 1$ nonlinear equations has to be solved.

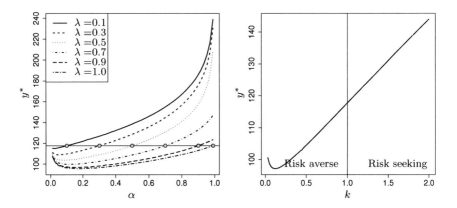

Figure 3.10: Optimal order quantity y^* for a mean-CVaR_α (left plot) and a power (right plot) risk spectrum objective function with shortage penalty cost. Note that the circles on the lines correspond to the risk-neutral y^* and for each line separate between risk-averse (left) and risk-seeking (right) behaviour.

3.3.3 Numerical study of the inventory control problem with shortage penalty cost

For the numerical analysis of the inventory control problem with shortage penalty cost we use the same set of parameters as with the numerics for the basic inventory problem in Section 3.2.3. Additionally, we assume a shortage penalty cost $s = 5$ unless otherwise noted.

Figure 3.10 shows the optimal order quantity in the level of risk aversion. Unlike the case of zero shortage penalty cost, now y^* is no longer monotone in the level of risk aversion. While the order quantity increases as the decision maker becomes risk-seeking, the order quantity is not non-increasing as the decision maker becomes more risk-averse. For some ranges of risk-aversion the quantity is reduced. However, as the decision maker becomes very risk-averse (the risk preference is extremely low), her focus turns towards reducing the impact of the very rare case where demand is extremely high and high shortage penalty cost are realized. Hence, the order quantity increases again.

Note that y^* goes to infinity as α or k gets closer to zero. In Figure 3.10 this property is not very clear, but if we increase the penalty cost to $s = 30$ this effect becomes more clear, as can be seen in Figure 3.11. Hence, we see that a risk-averse decision maker might order more than a risk-neutral one.

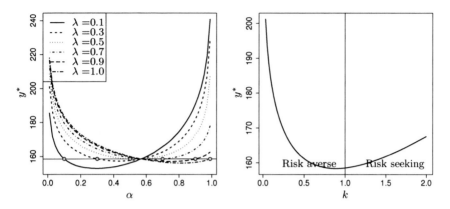

Figure 3.11: Optimal order quantity y^* for a mean-CVaR_α (left plot) and a power (right plot) risk spectrum objective function with large shortage penalty cost, $s = 30$.

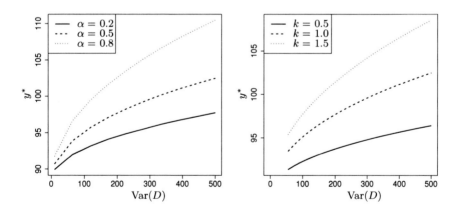

Figure 3.12: Optimal order quantity y^* for a mean-CVaR_α (left) and power (right) risk spectrum as a function of demand variance σ^2, where $D \sim \text{Gamma}(\mu, \sigma^2)$.

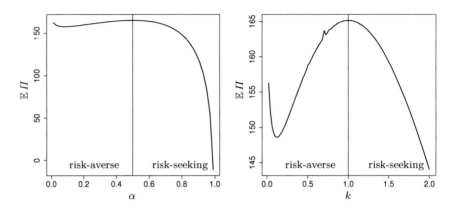

Figure 3.13: Expected profit with corresponding y^* for a mean-CVaR_α (left plot) and a power (right plot) risk spectrum with shortage penalty cost.

The effect of demand variance on y^* is shown in Figure 3.12. Similar to the case without penalty cost (see Figure 3.3), the difference between y^* with respect to risk aversion gets larger as variance increases. Note that for a risk-averse newsvendor, i.e. $\alpha = 0.2$ or $k = 0.5$, if there is no shortage penalty cost, y^* is decreasing in variance (see Figure 3.3), while now, when $s = 5$, it is increasing. However, this is not a general rule but depends on the cost parameters. For example, if the shortage penalty cost is decreased to $s = 3$, y^* is again decreasing in variance for $\alpha = 0.2$ and $k = 0.5$ as in the case of zero penalty cost.

In Figure 3.13 we illustrate the expected profit for a mean-CVaR_α and a power risk spectrum. The expected profit is maximized in the risk-neutral case and decreases once the decision maker becomes more risk-seeking. For the case of risk aversion, however, the expected profit is no longer monotone since the optimal order quantity is not monotone in the level of risk aversion as shown in Figure 3.10.

Figure 3.14 shows the 90% confidence interval and the maximum possible profit at y^* with respect to the level of risk aversion. In any case, the minimum possible profit is $-\infty$, and this causes the confidence interval to be larger compared to the zero penalty cost case. Specifically, for small α and k, when $s = 0$ the newsvendor is able to significantly decrease the difference between $\pi_{\max}$ and $\pi_{\min}$ by ordering very little and consequently achieving quite a tight CI (see Figure 3.5). However, here when $s > 0$, even

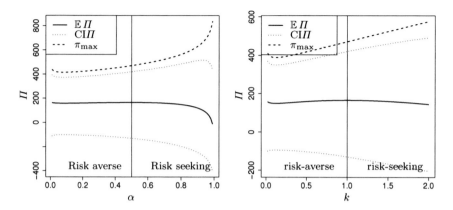

Figure 3.14: Expected profit with corresponding y^* for a mean-CVaR_α (left plot) and a power (right plot) risk spectrum with a 90% confidence interval CI Π and maximum profit $\pi_{\max}$. Note that minimum profit is $-\infty$.

when the newsvendor is very risk-averse, he is not able to reach such a small confidence interval.

Figure 3.15 depicts the probability of missing different profit target levels. Note that unlike the case without shortage penalty cost, PL_L has no jump at $(p - c)y$ anymore but is a continuous function. When using the optimal order quantity, the shape of PL_L is influenced by the shape of the optimal order quantity in the level of risk aversion as shown in Figure 3.10. The non-monotonicity of y^* causes the increasing-decreasing-increasing shape of PL_L, e.g. for $L = 150$.

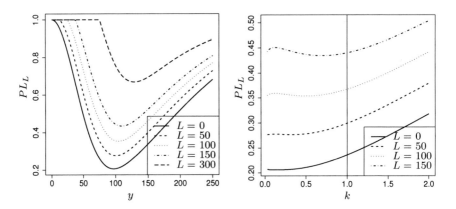

Figure 3.15: Probability of missing a profit target L, i.e. $\mathbb{P}(\Pi \leq L)$ with different order quantities (left) and with the degree of risk aversion k, where the corresponding optimal order quantity for a power risk spectrum is used.

3.4 Applications in supply chain management

So far in this chapter, we have discussed the inventory control problem from the view of a single decision maker, as when the newsvendor is a single entity or an agent in a supply chain. The problem can also be viewed from a supply chain perspective. When risk sensitivity is included in supply chain coordination issues, the complications are twofold: the optimal policies and coordinating contracts become more complicated, and the objective of the whole chain gets more difficult to describe. "When each of the agents maximizes his expected profit, the objective of the supply chain considered as a single entity is unambiguously to maximize its total expected profit (...). Regardless of the measure used, when one or more agents in the supply chain are risk-averse, it is no longer obvious as to what the objective function of the supply chain entity should be." (Gan et al., 2004).

Lau and Lau (1999) and Tsay (2002) focus on return policies concerning a single manufacturer and a single retailer who are both risk-averse. Lau and Lau (1999) assume both parties have mean-variance objective functions and all of the leftover inventory on the retailer's side can be returned to the manufacturer, so the policy parameter is just the salvage value and not the proportion of leftovers that can be returned. They obtain the optimal wholesale price and salvage value for normally distributed demand, but the optimality refers to maximizing the manufacturer's objective function. They show that as the manufacturer becomes more risk-averse, he sets both the salvage value and the wholesale price lower, which basically means that he tries to put more of the risk on retailers' shoulders. Since the problem is modeled from the side of the manufacturer the supply chain performance is not taken into account.

Tsay (2002) assumes a single manufacturer, single retailer setting, both maximizing their mean-standard deviation objective. The manufacturer sets the return policy and then the retailer sets his selling price after the uncertain demand is revealed. The demand distribution is modeled as a two-point distribution, i.e. low with probability ρ, high with $1 - \rho$. The policy is either a no-returns policy or a full-return for full-credit policy, so not a continuum as in Lau and Lau (1999). They find the equilibrium under each policy. In case there are no returns the manufacturer's risk sensitivity has no effect since there is no uncertainty on his side. When the retailer orders too few because of his risk aversion, the manufacturer lowers the wholesale price to increase the retailer's order. As a result, depending on the demand parameters, the retailer's risk aversion might cause his expected profit to increase because of the decreasing wholesale price. In case of full-return for full-credit, a retailer's risk sensitivity has no effect on the policy parameters, while depending on the degree of his risk aversion the manufacturer may lower the wholesale price when he accepts returns.

When the manufacturer is risk-neutral he increases the wholesale price if he accepts returns. However, returns make his profit more variable and one way to decrease variability is by decreasing the variability on sales. Hence, if he is risk-averse he lowers the wholesale price, which induces lower retail prices and smaller variability in profit. Hence, all else equal, the retailer should search for a risk-averse supplier.

Agrawal and Seshadri (2000) assume a risk-neutral manufacturer selling items to a number of newsvendors who differ in their risk sensitivity, which is measured by a mean-variance rule. Newsvendors operate in identical and independent markets and the selling price of the product is the same in each market. The manufacturer does not know the degree of risk aversion of each single newsvendor, but he knows the distribution of risk aversion among them. Under this setting they design a menu of contracts which should be offered by a risk-neutral intermediary who bares the risk of the newsvendors in different proportions depending on the contract that the newsvendor selects from the menu. Each contract in the menu includes a risky part which comes from the uncertain profit and a fixed side-payment from the intermediary to the newsvendor. The more risk-averse newsvendors select one of the contracts with a large side-payment. Chen and Seshadri (2006) prove the optimality of Agrawal and Seshadri's menu of contracts in the sense that it maximizes the intermediary's return, which means designing a setting that increases the order quantities to the optimal level in the risk-neutral case. However, as mentioned by the authors, if pricing is also considered, the existence of an intermediary might cause higher retail prices and lower consumption.

While Lau and Lau (1999) and Tsay (2002) do not mention coordination at all, Agrawal and Seshadri (2000) consider the total order quantity in the channel but none of them considers Pareto optimality.

Gan et al. (2004) are the first to examine coordinating contracts based on Pareto optimality with risk-averse agents. Their definition of supply chain coordination assumes "no agent's payoff can be improved without impairing someone else's payoff and each agent receives at least his reservation payoff." They differentiate between the channel's external and internal problem as the order/production quantities, and the allocation of profit. When there is at least one risk-neutral agent within the supply chain, as a Pareto optimal sharing rule, he can take all the risky profit and give side-payments to the other agents when the external decision is set to maximize the chain's expected profit. This statement is in line with the results of Agrawal and Seshadri (2000).

In order to develop coordinating contracts Gan et al. (2004) consider a supply chain with a single retailer and a single manufacturer. When both agents maximize their mean-variance tradeoffs, or an exponential utility function, the revenue-sharing contract and the buy-back contract can coordinate the chain if a side-payment to the retailer is included. If the manufacturer is risk-neutral it is Pareto optimal if he bears all the risk and just gives a fixed payment to the retailer. This result is extended by Chen et al. (2008a).

However, the results cannot be generalized to a concave utility function. They give an example where the manufacturer is risk-averse at low returns and risk-neutral at higher levels. For this specific example they show that neither the buy-back nor the revenue sharing contract can coordinate the channel since it is not possible to develop a proportional sharing rule. They mention that for general cases new contract forms should be designed.

Gan et al. (2005) study a supply chain with a risk-neutral manufacturer and a retailer who has a constraint on the probability of reaching a certain profit. The standard revenue-sharing and buy-back contracts do not coordinate the channel anymore. They construct a coordinating contract which is quite complicated compared to the contracts for expected profit maximizing agents.

Chen et al. (2008a) study a decentralized supply chain with multiple risk-neutral or risk-averse agents. They introduce the concept of rational contracts and analyze a supply chain with multiple risk-averse suppliers and a single risk-averse retailer. For the second case, the authors identify conditions of coordinating contracts and propose specific contracts based on the level of risk aversion among the suppliers and the retailer. Chen et al.'s contract includes fixed side-payments as mentioned by Gan et al. (2004) and also the concept of intermediaries mentioned by Agrawal and Seshadri (2000). They show that if the level of risk aversion is the same between all the players in the supply chain, any contract that coordinates the risk-neutral case coordinates this case as well. If the retailer and the manufacturers have different levels of risk aversion the type of the coordinating contract changes depending on who the least risk-averse player is.

Wang and Webster (2007) study supply chain coordination contracts between a single risk-neutral supplier and a single risk-averse retailer using a piecewise linear utility function as already discussed in Wang and Webster (2009). Their results indicate that coordinating contracts based on the assumption of risk neutrality may result in markedly lower supply chain profit when retailers are loss-averse; hence, suppliers should consider the impact of loss aversion in contract design, in particular when dealing with small retailers for whom the assumption of risk neutrality is less likely to hold.

Lastly, two papers on newsvendor networks by Tomlin and Wang (2005) and van Mieghem (2007) include risk aversion in the network design problem. Tomlin and Wang (2005) consider unreliable resources and uncertain demand. They show that for a risk-averse decision maker, dedicated sourcing may be more preferable than the flexible one. The only uncertainty in van Mieghem (2007) is the demand uncertainty and he shows that the risk-averse newsvendor may increase network capacity more than the risk-neutral one.

The main conclusions of the papers presented in this section are: when the agents with different degrees of risk aversion require different contracts, some of the coordinating contracts assuming risk neutrality do not work under risk aversion, and one way of dealing with this problem is introducing risk-neutral intermediaries into the channel. In the end, when risk aversion is considered, the contracts and/or the design of the supply chain become more complicated.

Chapter 4

Inventory & Pricing Problem with Risk Measures

While the inventory control problem with risk preferences has been intensively analyzed by different authors in different settings, this variety of models, approaches and results cannot be found for the combined inventory and pricing problem. Basically, only two important works have been published so far. Agrawal and Seshadri (2000) study a newsvendor problem with pricing within the expected utility framework, while Chen et al. (2009) analyze the problem under a CVaR_α objective function.

Agrawal and Seshadri (2000) consider general demand distributions for both additive and multiplicative uncertainties, using a concave utility function as objective. They show that the risk aversion affects the pricing decision differently depending on the relation of price and demand. Consequently, the ordering decision is also affected differently. Under multiplicative uncertainty, increase in risk aversion leads to an increase in price and decrease in quantity. Under additive uncertainty, risk aversion results in a decrease in price and the effect on quantity depends on the relation of the degree of risk aversion and the price elasticity of demand. Indeed, the opposite effect of risk aversion on price is not surprising. Independent of risk attitude, the demand variability is controlled by changing the price in different directions for different uncertainty models. The risk-averse newsvendor uses price as a hedge against demand uncertainty, but in opposite ways under the two uncertainty models. We will see that under some assumptions this effect also holds true for the case when spectral risk measures are used as objective functions.

In the following we discuss the properties of the inventory & pricing problem again under a spectral risk measure. While some of the properties of this problem can be found for any combination of the deterministic demand $d(p)$ and the stochastic error term E, for most of the analysis we need to specify this relation. Hence, in the following, we use the two most common combinations: the additive and the multiplicative demand models. Recall from introductory Section 1.1.2 that in the additive case, $D(p) = d(p) + E$, and in the multiplicative demand model, $D(p) = d(p)E$, where $d(p)$ denotes the deterministic price-dependent demand function, and E denote a price-independent demand error.

For the following analysis it is of great advantage if we do not consider the ordering decision y directly, but use a stocking factor z instead: in the additive model $y = d(p) + z$ and in the multiplicative model $y = d(p)z$. The transformation of the order quantity to a stocking factor was already used by Petruzzi and Dada (1999) for the analysis of the joint inventory & pricing problem under risk neutrality. If we define in this chapter F as the distribution function of demand *error* and f its density, then we can write the risk measure of profit from the stocking factor as

$$\mathrm{M}\big(\Pi_\epsilon(p, z)\big) = (p - c)z - (p - v) \int_{-\infty}^{z} \Phi\Big(F(\varepsilon)\Big) \, d\varepsilon. \qquad (4.1)$$

Recall from Definition 4 that translation equivariance of the risk measure implies $\mathrm{M}(X + a) = a + \mathrm{M}(X)$. Hence, using (1.10), for the risk measure of the additive demand model, we can write

$$\mathrm{M}\big(\Pi(p, y)\big) = \Pi_{\mathrm{Det}}(p) + \mathrm{M}\big(\Pi_\varepsilon(p, z)\big), \qquad (4.2)$$

where $\Pi_{\mathrm{Det}}(p)$ is the deterministic profit (a "sure" income) and $\mathrm{M}(\Pi_\varepsilon(p, z))$ denotes the risk measure of stochastic profit arising from demand error uncertainty. Note that $\Pi_{\mathrm{Det}}(p)$ is a function of price p only, as in the deterministic case the order quantity always equals demand, so $y = d(p)$ and $\Pi_{\mathrm{Det}}(p) = (p - c)d(p)$.

For the multiplicative demand model we take advantage of the positive homogeneity of the risk measure, $\mathrm{M}(\lambda X) = \lambda \mathrm{M}(X)$. By reformulating (1.11) we can write

$$\mathrm{M}\big(\Pi(p, y)\big) = d(p) \times \mathrm{M}\big(\Pi_\varepsilon(p, z)\big). \qquad (4.3)$$

Hence, the risk measure of the complete operation, i. e. the risk measure of $\Pi(p, y)$, can be decomposed into the factor $d(p)$, and the risk measure of stochastic profit made with the demand error $\Pi_\varepsilon(p, z)$.

For the joint optimization problem it does not make any difference if (p, y) or (p, z) is optimized as both formulations lead to the same p^*, and the optimal quantity depending on the demand model used, $y^* = d(p) + z^*$ in the additive and $y^* = d(p)z^*$. In the following analysis we use both ways of formulating the problem, we write the model based on y or z depending on whichever formulation is more convenient. Note, however, that structural properties of price differ if the optimal price for a constant y or for a constant z is analyzed. As far as possible, we try to formulate and analyze both cases.

4.1 The basic inventory & pricing problem

For the case that an explicit risk measure is used, we extend the results obtained in the literature so far by transforming the risk-averse or risk-seeking inventory & pricing problem into a risk-neutral problem. The idea behind this is that the application of any spectral risk measure can be seen as a transformation of the underlying demand distribution (see the discussion about rescaling the distribution function in Section 2.3.1). Once risk transformation functions Φ preserve certain properties of the demand distribution to the transformed distribution, any results found in the literature about the risk-neutral problem using those properties on the demand distribution also apply for the transformed problem under risk measures. In the following section we will describe these properties in more detail and show which risk transformation functions preserve them.

4.1.1 Necessary properties of the demand (error) distribution and risk spectra preserving them

An important property of distribution functions is the failure rate. Lariviere (2006) defines the failure rate (or hazard rate) of a random variable as follows:

Definition 8 (Failure rate). *Let X be a random variable with distribution function F and density f. Its failure rate is defined as*

$$h(x) = \frac{f(x)}{1 - F(x)}. \tag{4.4}$$

Moreover, we say the random variable has increasing failure rate (IFR) if $h'(x) \geq 0$ for all x.

Definition 9 (Generalized Failure rate). *Let X be a random variable with distribution function F and density f. Its generalized failure rate is defined as*

$$h^g(x) = \frac{xf(x)}{1 - F(x)}. \tag{4.5}$$

Moreover, we say the random variable has increasing generalized failure rate (IGFR) if $h^{g\prime}(x) \geq 0$ for all x.

Barlow and Proschan (1996) list distribution functions satisfying the IFR and IGFR property, respectively. Among them are the exponential, uniform, normal, truncated normal and subsets of Weibull or gamma distributions.

We can transform the problem under the risk measure to a standard risk-neutral problem by transforming the demand (error) distribution function with the risk transformation function. Recall from Section 1.1.1 that the expected value inventory problem can be written as

$$\mathbb{E}\,\Pi(y) = (p - c)y - (p - v) \int_0^y F(x)\,dx, \qquad (4.6)$$

which we reformulated later on in Section 3.2 for using risk measures as

$$\mathrm{M}(\Pi(y)) = (p - c)y - (p - v) \int_0^y \Phi(F(x))\,dx.$$

Note that instead of integrating the demand distribution directly, a risk-transformed distribution $F_\phi(x) := \Phi(F(x))$ with density $f_\phi(x) = \phi(F(x))f(x)$ is used. If we write

$$\mathrm{M}(\Pi(y)) = (p - c)y - (p - v) \int_0^y F_\phi(x)\,dx, \qquad (4.7)$$

it can be seen easily that the objective is identical with (4.6) and, hence, properties of the first problem hold as long as the necessary properties of F are preserved to F_ϕ. In particular, we need F_ϕ to have increasing failure rate for the later analysis of the inventory & pricing problem. Because of this reason, we analyze the common risk transformation functions, i.e. CVaR_α, mean-CVaR_α, power and exponential functions, and summarize the results in the following paragraphs.

Definition 10 (Risk transformation functions preserving IFR and IGFR). *Let the failure rate $h(x)$ and generalized failure rate $h_g(x)$ of the distribution F be increasing in x, and let F_ϕ be the risk-transformed distribution with density f_ϕ. We say a risk spectrum is* failure rate preserving *if the transformed failure rate*

$$h_\phi(x) = \frac{f_\phi(x)}{1 - F_\phi(x)} = \frac{f(x)\phi(F(x))}{1 - \Phi(F(x))} \qquad (4.8)$$

and the transformed generalized failure rate

$$h_\phi^g(x) = \frac{x f_\phi(x)}{1 - F_\phi(x)} = \frac{x f(x)\phi(F(x))}{1 - \Phi(F(x))} \qquad (4.9)$$

are increasing in x.

Lemma 7 (Examples of failure rate preserving risk spectra). *The* CVaR_α *risk spectrum as defined in (2.10) and the power risk spectrum as defined in (2.12) are failure rate preserving.*

Proof.

1. CVaR_α risk spectrum: The transformed distribution is $F_\phi(x) = \frac{1}{\alpha} F(x)$ for any $F(x) < \alpha$. Plugging in for the failure rate results in

$$h_\phi(x) = \frac{f(x)}{\alpha - F(x)},$$

such that

$$h_\phi(x) = h(x) \times \frac{1 - F(x)}{\alpha - F(x)}.$$

Since the second term is increasing in x for any $\alpha < 1$ and the failure rate $h(x)$ is increasing in x by definition, $h_\phi(x)$ is increasing in x for $x < F^{-1}(\alpha)$. For any $x \geq F^{-1}(\alpha)$, the distribution $F_\phi(x) = 1$.

2. Power risk spectrum: For $\phi(\omega) = \frac{1}{k}(1 - \omega)^{\frac{1}{k} - 1}$ and $\Phi(\omega) = 1 - (1 - \omega)^{\frac{1}{k}}$ the failure rate of the risk-transformed distribution is

$$h_\phi(x) = h(x) \times \frac{1}{k}.$$

Hence $h_\phi(x)$ is increasing in x if $h(x)$ is increasing in x.

□

Note that the two other commonly used risk spectra, the mean-CVaR_α and the exponential risk spectrum, do not preserve IFR as can be seen from Figure 4.1. Especially for the case of a mean-CVaR_α risk spectrum the transformed failure rate $h_\phi(x)$ has a downward jump at $\omega = F^{-1}(\alpha)$, exactly where the risk spectrum $\phi(\omega)$ changes its level from $\frac{\lambda}{\alpha}$ to $\frac{1 - \lambda}{1 - \alpha}$.

4.1.2 Results for the joint optimal inventory & pricing problem

Here we present properties of the inventory & pricing problem for both additive and multiplicative demand models based on the IFR preserving property as discussed above. An important result concerns the joint-unimodality in price and order quantity. After deriving this we present structural properties of the joint-optimal controls in certain parameters, such as level of risk

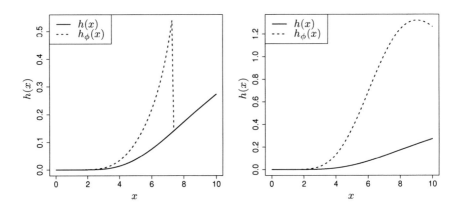

Figure 4.1: Failure rate $h(x)$ and risk-transformed failure rate $h_\phi(x)$ for a mean-CVaR$_\alpha$ (left) and exponential (right) risk spectrum. It can be seen that the risk-transformed distribution F_ϕ does not show the IFR property anymore, although the distribution F has IFR.

aversion, cost and salvage value parameters. In Section 4.1.3 we will analyze the pricing-only problem for either a given order quantity or a given stocking factor. Clearly, structural results for the single-dimensional optimization will differ from the joint-optimization problem. To clearly distinguish between the two cases, in the following we will denote by p^*, y^*, and z^* the joint optimal controls, while the optimal price for a given quantity or stocking factor will be denoted by $p^*(y)$ and $p^*(z)$, respectively. Note that we do not analyze the behaviour of $y^*(p)$ and $z^*(p)$ in detail, as this refers to the inventory-only problem which was discussed already in Chapter 3.

An important result of the (risk-neutral) price-setting newsvendor problem was obtained by Yao et al. (2006). They show that for a certain class of demand functions, the expected profit is unimodal (quasi-concave) in both price and quantity. In particular, if the deterministic demand has increasing price elasticity (IPE) and the random term has increasing failure rate (IFR), then the expected profit is unimodal.

Let $\epsilon(p)$ denote the price elasticity of demand $d(p)$, then $\epsilon(p) = -\frac{pd'(p)}{d(p)}$. Note that the price elasticity is the relative change of demand for a relative change in price. We can state the following:

Definition 11 (IPE). *A deterministic demand function $d(p)$ has increasing price elasticity (IPE), if*

$$\frac{d\epsilon}{dp} \geq 0 \quad \text{for all } p. \tag{4.10}$$

Yao et al. (2006) give an intuitive explanation: "As the price increases by a certain percentage, the demand decreases by a larger percentage, which makes it less desirable to raise the price further." They further show that for a wide range of important demand functions such as

1. linear $d(p) = a(p_{\max} - p)$;

2. power $d(p) = (1 + p)^{-a}$ for $a > 1$;

3. exponential $d(p) = p^{-a}e^{-\lambda p}$ for $a > 0$, $\lambda > 0$; or

4. iso-elastic $d(p) = p^{-a}$ for $a > 1$

functions, among others, the IPE property holds.

Combining the result of Yao et al. (2006) with spectral risk measures leads to the following proposition about the unimodality of the risk measure in price and quantity, (p, y). Note, however, that as discussed in the introduction of this chapter, we will decompose the demand into its deterministic part and the stochastic demand error. We assume the distribution of the error term, $F(\varepsilon)$, is continuous with density $f(\varepsilon)$ and invertible, so $F^{-1}(F(\varepsilon)) = \varepsilon$.

Proposition 9 (Unimodality of the risk measure with respect to price and quantity). *Let $\phi(\omega)$ be an admissible risk spectrum. The corresponding risk measure $M(\Pi(p, y))$ is jointly unimodal (quasi-concave) in (p, y) if*

1. the demand error has an increasing failure rate (IFR), or the demand error is a positive random variable and has an increasing generalized failure rate (IGFR), and

2. mean demand $\mathbb{E} D(p)$ has increasing price elasticity (IPE), and

3. the risk transformation function $\Phi(\omega)$ preserves IFR or IGFR, respectively.

Proof. Part (a) and (b) of Proposition 9 were shown by Yao et al. (2006), so as long as (c) holds, the problem can be transformed into a risk-neutral problem and properties already found in the literature of the risk-neutral solution can be used. □

It is common to assume, without loss of generality, that the mean demand error is 0 for the additive model and 1 for the multiplicative model. Any mean different from these values can be easily captured by a transformation of the deterministic demand function. Hence, we assume that the demand error distribution of an additive model has negative and positive support, while the distribution for the multiplicative model has only a positive support. For the rest of this section we assume that the demand error distribution and the risk transformation function satisfy the conditions stated in Proposition 9, unless otherwise stated.

Note that unlike the optimal order quantity in the inventory problem, no explicit formulation of optimal price p^* for a general distribution and general risk spectrum can be found. For the joint price-quantity optimization in the case of an additive demand model, a single-dimensional numerical search of the maximum risk measure on price is indeed possible on

$$M(\Pi(p)) = (p - c)d(p) + (p - c)z^*(p) - (p - v) \int_{-d(p)}^{z^*(p)} F_\phi(\varepsilon)\,d\varepsilon. \quad (4.11)$$

When the demand model is of multiplicative form, the search must be carried out on

$$M(\Pi(p)) = d(p) \left[(p - c)z^*(p) - (p - v) \int_0^{z^*(p)} F_\phi(\varepsilon)\,d\varepsilon \right]. \quad (4.12)$$

where the optimal stocking factor for both formulations is

$$z^*(p) = \Phi^{-1}\left(F\left(\frac{p - c}{p - v} \right) \right).$$

Since the problems in (4.11) and (4.12) are unimodal in their arguments and have a lower bound on price, i.e. $p^* > c$, a numerical optimization using standard single dimensional optimization techniques is still very efficient.

An immediately following results concerns the monotonicity of optimal price p^* with respect to cost c.

Proposition 10 (Monotonicity of the optimal controls p^* and y^* with respect to c). *If the mean demand $\mathbb{E}\,D$ has IPE, the distribution of demand error, F, has IFR, and the risk spectrum is failure rate preserving,*

1. *then the risk measure of profit,* $M(\Pi(p,y))$ *is strictly supermodular[1] in* (p^*, c), *so that the optimal price* p^* *is increasing in cost* c;

2. *the optimal critical fractile* CSL^* *is decreasing in* c, *i. e.* $\frac{dCSL^*}{dc} \leq 0$, *where the equality holds for iso-elastic* $d(p)$;

3. *the optimal order quantity* y^* *is strictly decreasing in* c.

Proof. Yao et al. (2006) showed that the IPE and IFR properties are sufficient for the risk-neutral problem. If, in addition, the risk spectrum is failure rate preserving, the problem can be transformed into a risk-neutral problem such that the sufficient properties still hold. □

With respect to salvage value we are not able to derive general structural results for both demand formulations. While p^* and y^* are monotone in the salvage value for the additive model, this no longer holds for the multiplicative demand formulation. The reason why the behaviour is not necessarily monotone is that while both price and quantity tend to increase in salvage value, the increase of each of the two controls has the opposite effect on the other. The increasing price due to the increase in salvage value leads to a decrease of $d(p)$, which causes the order quantity to decrease. This is in contradiction to the direct effect of the salvage value on quantity for a given price, hence the resulting behaviour depends on whichever effect dominates. We can summarize these findings in the following:

Proposition 11 (Monotonicity of p^* with respect to v). *If, for an additive demand model, the mean demand,* $\mathbb{E}\,D$, *has IPE, the distribution of demand error,* F, *has IFR, and the risk spectrum is failure rate preserving,*

1. *the risk measure of profit,* $M(\Pi(p,y))$ *is strictly supermodular in* (p^*, v), *so that the optimal price* p^* *is increasing in* v;

2. *the optimal critical fractile* CSL^* *and the optimal stocking factor* z^* *are increasing in* v.

See Appendix A for a proof. Chen et al. (2009) previously derived the results for the specific case of the $CVaR_\alpha$ risk spectrum, where for the multiplicative demand model a monotonicity result can also be found if

---

[1]A continuous, differentiable function $f(x,y)$ is supermodular, if and only if its cross derivative is positive, $\frac{\partial^2 f(x,y)}{\partial x \partial y} \geq 0$. Topkis (1998) showed that a positive cross partial derivative implies that the optimal $x^*(y)$ is increasing in y. If $\frac{\partial^2 f(x,y)}{\partial x \partial y} \leq 0$, $f(x,y)$ is submodular and $x^*(y)$ decreases in y.

salvage value is sufficiently small. Unfortunately, we are not able to find monotonicity results about the behaviour of y^* with respect to v in the additive model for a general risk spectrum. For a $CVaR_\alpha$ risk spectrum, Chen et al. (2009) are able to show that y^* is strictly increasing in v.

Proposition 12 (Monotonicity of p^* with respect to the level of risk aversion, η). *Let η denote the risk preference according to Definition 7.*

1. *For an additive demand model, the risk measure of profit is supermodular in (p^*, η), hence, p^* is increasing in η.*

2. *For a multiplicative demand model, if $H(\varepsilon) := \frac{x f_\phi(\varepsilon)}{\frac{\partial}{\partial \eta} F_\phi(\varepsilon, \eta)}$ is increasing in ε, then p^* is increasing in η, and if $H(\varepsilon)$ is decreasing in ε, then p^* is decreasing in η.*

See Appendix A for a proof. Note that this additional technical assumption for the specific case of a $CVaR_\alpha$ decision maker reduces to $\left(\frac{F(\varepsilon)}{\varepsilon f(\varepsilon)} \right)' > 0$, which was found by Chen et al. (2009) as an additional assumption for p^* being increasing in η for the multiplicative demand model.

Based on the monotonicity result of the optimal price we can immediately derive monotonicity results for the optimal cycle service level and the optimal stocking factor in the following:

Corollary 5 (Monotonicity of CSL^* and z^* in η). *The optimal cycle service level*

$$CSL^* = \Phi^{-1} \left(\frac{p^* - c}{p^* - v} \right) \qquad (4.13)$$

is increasing in η, if the optimal price p^* is increasing in η. This also implies that the optimal stocking factor $z^* = F^{-1}(CSL^*)$ is increasing in η.

Proof. Recall from Definition 6(b) that Φ decreases in η and Φ^{-1} increases in η. By p^* increasing in η, $CSL^* = \Phi^{-1} \left(\frac{p^* - c}{p^* - v} \right)$ increases in η since $v < c$ by definition, and consequently $z^* = F^{-1}(CSL^*)$ increases in η. $\square$

Note that this monotonicity result of p^*, CSL^* and z^* specifically for the $CVaR_\alpha$ risk spectrum was found previously by Chen et al. (2009).

If we want to understand the behaviour of the optimal order quantity y^*, we need to consider two opposite effects induced by the change of the level of risk aversion. On the one hand, the decreasing deterministic demand $d(p)$ due to higher optimal prices in η suggests a lower order quantity; on the other hand there is the opposite effect of the increasing optimal stocking factor $z(p^*)$. Hence, a monotonicity result of y^* with respect to η cannot be stated, as the optimal policy depends on whichever effect dominates. In the following numerical analysis in Section 4.1.4, Figure 4.3 shows an example of such a non-monotone behavior of the order quantity in the level of risk aversion.

4.1.3 Results for the pricing-only problem

After having discussed the behaviour of the problem in the joint-optimum price and quantity, we can derive additional structural properties of optimal price for a given quantity or a given stocking factor.

Proposition 13 (Monotonicity of optimal price $p^*(y)$). *If the distribution of demand error F has IFR and the risk spectrum is failure-rate preserving, the optimal price $p^*(y)$ is decreasing in the order quantity y.*

See Appendix A for a proof. Note that this result is in line with the findings of the risk-neutral model as found, for example, in Kocabıyıkoğlu and Popescu (2009) and Arıkan and Jammernegg (2009). The optimal price with respect to the stocking factor can be derived in the following:

Corollary 6. *The optimal price $p^*(z)$ is increasing in the stocking factor z.*

See Appendix A for a proof.

Corollary 7. *The optimal price $p^*(z, \eta)$ for a given stocking factor z is*

1. increasing in η for the additive demand model, and

2. decreasing in η for the multiplicative demand model.

See Appendix A for a proof.

This is a particularly interesting result. Two common ways of assessing the variability of a random variable, in particular when assessing demand, are the variance, $\text{Var}(D(p))$, and the coefficient of variation, $\text{CV}(D(p)) = \frac{\text{SD}(D(p))}{\mathbb{E} D(p)}$. Petruzzi and Dada (1999) already describe that the impact on demand variability of a price change for the risk-neutral setting has an opposite direction for the additive and the multiplicative models. In the additive model, demand variance $\text{Var}(D(p)) = \text{Var}(E)$ does not depend on price and $\text{CV}(D(p)) = \frac{\text{SD}(E)}{d(p) + \mathbb{E} E}$ increases in p. The variability for the multiplicative model has the opposite behavior: demand variance $\text{Var}(D(p)) = d(p) \, \text{Var}(E)$ is decreasing in p, while the coefficient of variation $\text{CV}(D(p)) = \frac{d(p) \, \text{SD}(E)}{d(p) \, \mathbb{E} E}$ is constant in price.

Mills (1959) shows for the additive model that the optimal price of a deterministic demand situation is always larger than the optimal price under demand uncertainty, while Karlin and Carr (1962) show the opposite behaviour for a newsvendor with multiplicative demand model. Therefore, the optimal price of a deterministic demand situation is always smaller than under demand uncertainty. Hence, in both models, the newsvendor uses price to reduce demand variability. We can observe a similar behaviour for risk-averse newsvendors with respect to the degree of risk aversion. From Corollary 7 we see that for a fixed stocking factor in the additive demand model, the optimal price decreases the more risk-averse a newsvendor becomes, and for the multiplicative model the optimal price increases the more risk-averse a newsvendor becomes. Hence, when getting more risk-averse, both use price to reduce demand variability (either the variance or the coefficient of variation).

4.1.4 Numerical study of the basic inventory & pricing problem

In this section we present a numerical study of the inventory & pricing problem in order to illustrate the findings introduced in the previous section and we discuss some of the structural properties of the problem in more detail. Furthermore, we can look at properties where no explicit analytic solution or structural properties could be found. In the following we present interesting aspects and properties of the problems analyzed. In this section we only consider IFR and IGFR preserving risk spectra, respectively, in particular the power risk spectrum. Additionally, in Section 4.1.5, we pay special attention to the mean-CVaR$_\alpha$ risk spectrum.

We use the following parameters for the analysis unless otherwise noted: production cost $c = 2$, salvage value $v = 1$, and no shortage penalty costs are considered (see Section 4.2 for numerics with positive shortage penalty cost). As demand model we use for the

- *multiplicative* model: $D(p) = 1000p^{-2}\varepsilon$ with $E \sim \text{Gamma}(1, 0.8)$, and for the

- *additive* demand model the linear function $d(p) = 100 - 10p$ with $E \sim \text{N}(0, 20)$.

Note that the criterion $H(\varepsilon)$, as defined in Proposition 12(b), for the Gamma distribution in the multiplicative model is increasing for $\text{Var}(E) < 1$ and decreasing for $\text{Var}(E) > 1$ and $\mathbb{E}\,E = 1$.

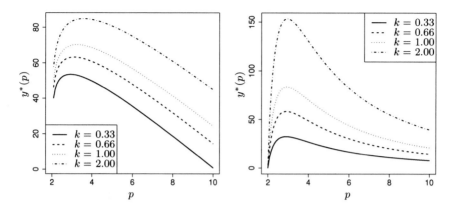

Figure 4.2: Optimal order quantity as a function of price, $y^*(p)$. Additive (left) and multiplicative demand model (right).

Non-monotonicity of $y^*(p)$ for additive and multiplicative models

In Figure 4.2 we see that for both the additive and the multiplicative models the optimal order quantity is non-monotone in price, so $y^*(p)$ is first increasing and then decreasing in p. This non-monotonicity comes from two opposing effects of the increase in price as described in Arıkan et al. (2007). On the one hand, a larger price increases the profitability of the product, meaning that the critical fractile $\frac{p-c}{p-v}$ increases such that the quantity tends to increase. On the other hand, the increase in price leads to a decrease of expected demand, which naturally should have a decreasing effect on the order quantity. As a consequence, for small prices the order quantity increases as the first effect dominates, and decreases for higher prices, since the second effect dominates for larger prices.

By numerically comparing different parameter sets it seems that the price up to which $y^*(p)$ is increasing is not very sensitive to the level of risk aversion, specifically for the multiplicative demand model. The optimal quantity for a given price changes dramatically with η.

Note that high prices in the additive model lead to unexpected behaviour. If we define the reservation price of a product p_r such that the deterministic demand at this price $d(p_r) = 0$, we see that the order quantity at p_r, depending on the level of risk aversion, is still clearly different from zero. The reason is that demand variance is independent of price, so also for any $p \geq p_r$ the newsvendor orders a positive, and in fact constant, quantity, just to take advantage of the demand error. This response is somewhat unsatisfactory on a practical level, since it implies a completely price-independent probabilistic demand. As a consequence, the additive model should only be applied when prices are small such that the corresponding demand is sufficiently large. To model the demand behaviour with high prices and low demand levels the multiplicative model is generally a better choice.

Behaviour of y^* in η for additive and multiplicative model

In the discussion following Corollary 5 we described that the behaviour of the joint optimal order quantity y^* in η is non-monotone since it depends on whether the effect of the decreasing demand in price or the increasing quantity due to a less risk-averse preference dominates. In general, the numerical analysis shows that for an extremely risk-averse newsvendor ($\eta \to 0$), the order quantity decreases to zero ($y^* \to 0$), as this allows her to reduce the risk to its minimum. Hence, y^* is necessarily increasing in η for small η. Depending on the demand model, the increase can be monotone, or up to a certain level of η. An analysis of different parameters suggests that for an additive linear demand model, y^* is increasing in η; the same result could be found for any multiplicative demand model. Only for an additive power demand model were we able to find non-monotone y^* behaviour as illustrated in Figure 4.3.

We need to comment further on the additive power demand model. As we showed in Proposition 12(a), p^* is increasing in η. At some level of η price is large enough such that the demand effect of the deterministic demand part vanishes and the price-independent demand error contributes most to profit. In this case, y^* is increasing in η.

For the multiplicative demand model we can distinguish two cases depending on the criterion $H(\varepsilon)$: If H is increasing in its argument, from Proposition 12(b) p^* is increasing in η, which causes mean demand to decrease and the profitability of the product to increase. However, as we see in the Figure 4.4, η has a very small effect on p^*. As we know from the inventory-only problem, $y^*(p)$ for a given p increases in η. By the numerical study we can observe that the latter effect dominates because the pricing effect is very small so that y^* is increasing in η.

When $H(\varepsilon)$ decreases, p^* decreases in η, so that mean demand increases and the profitability decreases. Changes in η do have stronger impact on p^* in this case. The increase in mean demand and the increase in $y^*(p)$ for a given p clearly dominate the loss of profitability of the product such that y^* is again increasing in η, even at a larger rate than in the case of increasing $H(\varepsilon)$.

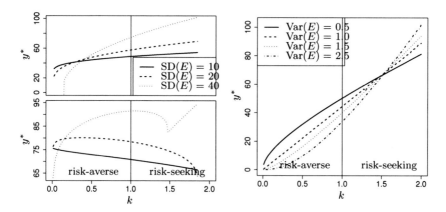

Figure 4.3: Joint optimal order quantity y^* for two additive (left) and multiplicative (right) demand models. The additive models differ in the deterministic demand function: linear demand, $d(p) = 100 - 10p$ (left up) and power demand, $d(p) = 1000p^{-2}$ (left bottom).

Monotonicity of p^* for the multiplicative model

While p^* is monotonically increasing in η for the additive model as shown in Proposition 12(a), the behaviour for the multiplicative model is not that clear. In part (b) of the same proposition we found a criterion $H(\varepsilon)$ defined on the risk-transformed distribution function such that p^* is increasing in η if $H(\varepsilon)$ increases in its argument, and vice versa. Figure 4.4 illustrates this relationship: for high demand variance the criterion is strictly decreasing, so that p^* is decreasing in η; for low values of demand error variance the criterion increases and, hence, $p^*(y)$ also increases. For the special case that the criterion is constant (dashed plot), p^* does not change with η.

The reason for this behavior is similar to the discussion on Corollary 7. The variance of demand in the multiplicative demand model depends on price, since $\text{Var}(D(p)) = \text{Var}(d(p)\varepsilon) = d(p)^2 \text{Var}(E)$. Hence, it is possible to decrease demand variance by increasing price. Whenever error variance is large, and therefore has a significant impact on the overall performance, as the newsvendor becomes more risk-averse he uses price to reduce demand variance compared to the risk-neutral case. Recall that in contrast to this, the demand variance in the additive model is constant in price, but the coefficient of variation $cv = \frac{\text{SD}(D(p))}{\mathbb{E} D(p)}$ increases in price. Hence, the risk-averse newsvendor with an additive demand model decreases price, again to reduce demand variability.

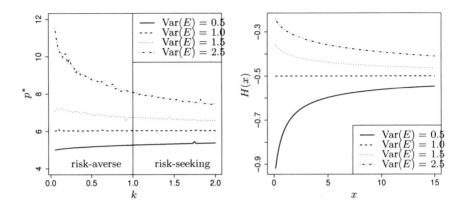

Figure 4.4: Joint optimal price p^* (left) for multiplicative demand models and the correspondig $H(\varepsilon)$ (right) from Proposition 12(b) for different variances of demand error.

Analyzing the effect of different values of k specifically for the power risk spectrum, we see that only the scaling but not the shape of $H(\varepsilon)$ changes with k, so whether or not $H(\varepsilon)$ for this formulation is increasing or decreasing does not depend on k.

Expected profit and confidence intervals

We illustrate in Figure 4.5 the expected profit of a newsvendor with multiplicative demand model and power risk spectrum for different risk aversion levels. Clearly the maximum expected profit is obtained for the risk-neutral parameters. The level of η has a considerable effect on the confidence interval of profit: while the expected profit decreases compared to the risk-neutral case as the decision maker becomes more risk-averse, the confidence interval gets tighter. In the case where the decision maker is risk-seeking, the opposite effect becomes true: the expected profit is decreasing compared to the risk-neutral case, and the confidence interval gets broader, which implies higher possible profit realizations for the risk-seeking newsvendor. A similar behaviour can be found if the underlying demand model has an additive structure.

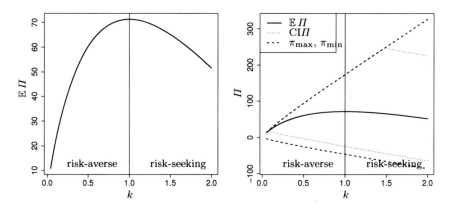

Figure 4.5: Expected profit (left) and 80% confidence interval with maximum/minimum profit realizations (right) for multiplicative demand model.

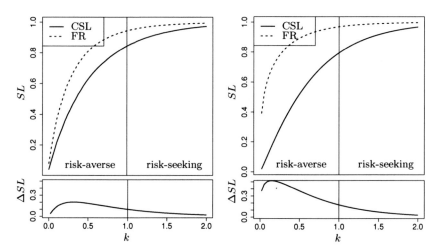

Figure 4.6: CSL and FR in η for joint optimal (p^*, y^*) for multiplicative (left) with $\text{Var}(E) = 2$ such that $H(\varepsilon)$ is decreasing and additive (right) demand model. Under each plot the difference $\Delta SL = FR - CSL$ is shown.

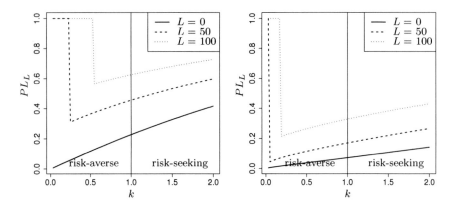

Figure 4.7: Probability of missing a profit target, $PL_L(\eta)$ for joint optimal (p^*, y^*) for multiplicative (left) and additive (right) demand models.

Customer service levels with respect to η

As we discussed earlier, customer service levels are important externally-oriented (customer-oriented) performance measures. In Figure 4.6 both the cycle service level (CSL) and the fill rate (FR) are shown in the level of risk preference η. As we already know from Corollary 5, for the additive demand model and multiplicative with increasing $H(\varepsilon)$, CSL is increasing in η. If, for the latter, $H(\varepsilon)$ is decreasing, i. e. p^* is decreasing in η, then the effect of increasing demand dominates the decrease in profitability so that CSL remains increasing in η.

Overall, our numerical analysis shows that, independent of the demand model formulation, both the cycle service level and the fill rate are increasing in η, although we are not able to find an analytical proof for this behaviour. Hence, a newsvendor might not only consider behaving in a risk-seeking way because of the chance for higher profit realizations, but also to increase his service levels. According to this analysis we can further comment that the differences between CSL and FR are larger for the risk-averse than for the risk-seeking newsvendor.

Probability of missing a profit target with respect to η

Similar to the discussion of the inventory-only problem in Chapter 3 we can now also consider the probability of missing a profit target PL_L at level L as an internally, cost-oriented performance measure. In Figure 4.7 we

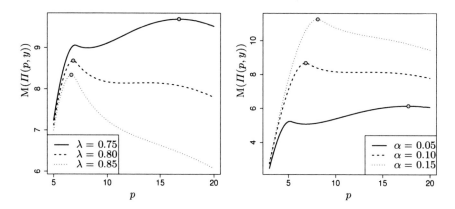

Figure 4.8: Optimal pricing problem for a newsvendor with mean-CVaR$_\alpha$ risk spectrum, fixed order quantity $y = 3$, multiplicative demand model with $d(p) = 1000p^{-2}$ and demand error $\sim$ Gamma$(1, 0.8)$, fixed $\alpha = 0.1$ (left) and fixed $\lambda = 0.8$ (right). The dots indicate the corresponding optimal prices.

show the behavior for both demand models. As in the case without pricing, the minimal PL_L is found for (p, y) such that these controls lead to the the maximum possible profit. For both demand models, PL_0 is strictly increasing in η with $PL_0 = 0$ in the limit of $\eta \to 0$. In this case, the optimal quantity $q^* \to 0$, so that the resulting profit is zero without any variability. For any $L > 0$, a very risk-averse newsvendor might find (p^*, z^*) such that L cannot be reached at all, even if $\varepsilon = z$.

4.1.5 Analysis of the mean-CVaR risk spectrum

In this section we are specifically interested in the mean-CVaR$_\alpha$ risk spectrum. The reason for this is twofold. On the one hand, mean-CVaR$_\alpha$ formulations are the most common extensions of the basic CVaR$_\alpha$ problem in the literature. On the other hand, some problematic issues arise when a mean-CVaR$_\alpha$ risk spectrum is applied to an inventory & pricing optimization due to its lack of the IFR or IGFR preserving property. Since this condition, as specified in Proposition 9, is no longer satisfied, the unimodality of the risk measure of profit is not guaranteed, as illustrated in Figure 4.8.

As can be seen from Figure 4.8, the risk measure of profit for a mean-CVaR$_\alpha$ risk spectrum is not necessarily unimodal in price, due to the non-increasing transformed failure rate. As the plots show, there can be a local maximum in the range of prices, where the correspondig $CSL < \alpha$, so

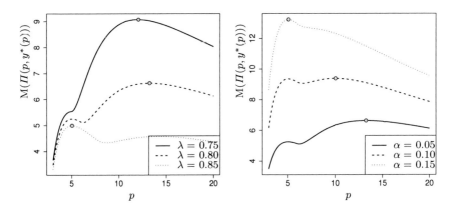

Figure 4.9: Optimal pricing problem where the newsvendor applies $y^*(p)$, multiplicative demand with $d(p) = 1000p^{-2}$, demand error $\sim$ Gamma$(1, 0.8)$, fixed $\alpha = 0.1$ (left) and fixed $\lambda = 0.8$ (right). The dots indicate the corresponding optimal prices.

the level of risk spectrum in the optimal price is $\frac{\lambda}{\alpha}$. Another local maximum can be for higher price ranges with correspondig $CSL > \alpha$, where $\phi = \frac{1-\lambda}{1-\alpha}$. Whichever local maximum is the global depends on the parameters of the risk spectra (compare solid and dashed/dotted plot). So, not only is the optimization problem no longer unimodal, but there is no relationship where one of the modes always dominates. However, our numerical analysis suggests that there are at most two modes in the optimization problem. If we order the optimal quantity $y^*(p)$ for each price, the optimization problem is still not unimodal as illustrated in Figure 4.9.

As Figure 4.10 shows, the optimal order quantity for the mean-CVaR$_\alpha$ risk spectrum reacts in a very special way to price. While the optimal quantity is first increasing and then decreasing in price for the CVaR$_\alpha$ and power risk spectra (Sec. 4.1.4), now $y^*(p)$ is increasing and decreasing twice because of the sharp jump at α in the risk spectrum. Recall from (3.13) that

$$y^*(p) = \begin{cases} F^{-1}\left(\frac{\alpha}{\lambda}\frac{p-c}{p-v}\right) & \frac{p-c}{p-v} \leq \lambda \\ F^{-1}\left(\frac{p-c}{p-v} + \frac{\alpha-\lambda}{1-\lambda}\frac{c-v}{p-v}\right) & \text{otherwise.} \end{cases}$$

Hence, in the range of p such that $\frac{p-c}{p-v} \leq \lambda$, we observe the increasing and decreasing shape of $y^*(p)$, as we discussed in the previous section for Figure 4.2. At $\frac{p-c}{p-v} = \lambda$, the risk spectrum changes from $\frac{\lambda}{\alpha}$ to the lower level

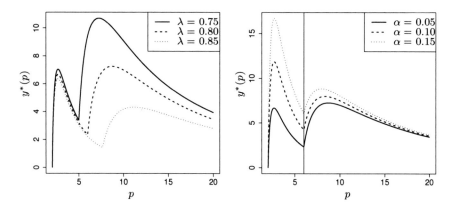

Figure 4.10: Optimal quantity $y^*(p)$, multiplicative demand model, $d(p) = 1000p^{-2}$, demand error $\sim$ Gamma$(1, 0.8)$ for $\alpha = 0.1$ and with different λ parameters (left) and $\lambda = 0.8$ and different α parameters (right).

$\frac{1-\lambda}{1-\alpha}$. As a consequence, for prices larger than, but still in the neighborhood of, this limit, the first effect again dominates. Due to the lower level of the risk spectrum the increase in profitability is now valued or considered more than before, so that optimal quantity is again increasing in price. Clearly, at some high price levels the first effect diminishes and the second effect dominates so that, ultimately, the order quantity is decreasing in price.

4.2 The inventory & pricing problem with shortage penalty cost

The joint inventory & pricing problem with positive shortage penalty and with consideration of the risk preferences is the most challenging problem, technically. To our knowledge, no analytical results exist in the literature yet. Unfortunately, we are also unable to derive analytical results. Hence, we need to rely on a comprehensive numerical study in order to gain insights into this problem. As we did for the previous sections, we will use standard parameters unless otherwise noted in the respective plots. In particular, we will use the same set of parameters, distribution functions and risk spectra as in Section 4.1.4, except that we will now assume shortage penalty cost $s = 5$.

Taking advantage of the translation equivariance of the spectral risk measure, we are able to formulate the additive problem as

$$M(\Pi(p, y)) = (p - c)d(p) + (p - c)z - (p - v) \int_{-\infty}^{z} G_\phi(\varepsilon) \, d\varepsilon, \qquad (4.14)$$

where $G_\phi(\varepsilon) = \Phi(G(\varepsilon)) = \Phi\left(F(\varepsilon) + 1 - F(\bar{\varepsilon})\right)$ and $\bar{\varepsilon} = z + (z - \varepsilon)\frac{p-v}{s}$ similar to (3.18) and Proposition 8. Due to positive homogeneity we can write the multiplicative problem as

$$M(\Pi(p, y)) = d(p) \left[(p - c)z - (p - v) \int_{0}^{z} G_\phi(\varepsilon) \, d\varepsilon \right]. \qquad (4.15)$$

In the following, we first analyze the unimodality of the problem with respect to price. Afterwards, we analyze structural properties of the optimal controls (p^*, y^*) with respect to η, considering different parameter sets. An analysis of performance indicators such as expected profit, confidence intervals of profit, service level measures and the probability of missing a profit target conclude the section on the inventory & pricing problem with shortage penalty costs.

4.2.1 Joint optimality and unimodality

As with the problem without shortage penalty costs, we look at the failure rate and generalized failure rate of F_ϕ for the additive and multiplicative models, respectively. The corresponding plots are shown in Figure 4.11. However, it is important to notice that neither rate is purely dependent on the demand distribution anymore, but they also depend on the parameters of the problem, since we model the effect of shortage penalty costs by a transformation of the demand distribution function. So, in particular for each price, the failure rate or generalized failure rate is different. Due to this dependency on price, IFR or IGFR is not necessarily sufficient for a unimodal behaviour in price, meaning it is no longer sufficient for having a single optimal price. Hence, we need to look at the risk measure of profit with respect to price specifically. Nonetheless, our numerical analysis shows that when applying admissible risk spectra (according to Definition 5) for different paramter sets, the IFR and IGFR properties preserve.

The optimal pricing problem, when numerically analyzed with various distribution functions for admissible risk spectra such as power or CVaR$_\alpha$ risk spectra, results in a unimodal optimization problem as in Figure 4.12.

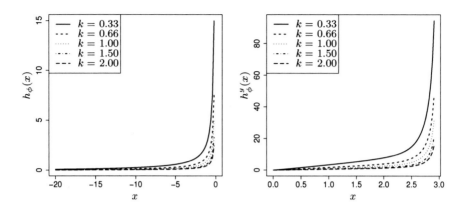

Figure 4.11: Failure rate (left) for the additive model and generalized failure rate (right) for the multiplicative model of the transformed distribution with a power risk spectrum for different values of risk preference parameter k. See (2.12) for the definition of the risk spectrum.

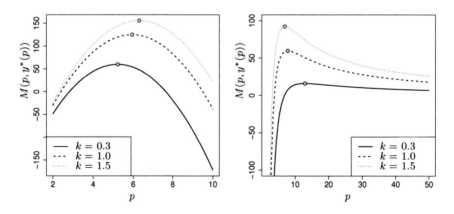

Figure 4.12: Risk measure of profit in price for additive (left) and multiplicative (right) demand models with a power risk spectrum. The dots mark the optimal prices.

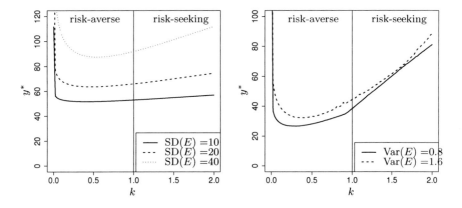

Figure 4.13: Joint optimal y^* for different levels of demand variability with additive (left) and multiplicative (right) demand model with a power risk spectrum.

We were not able to find a single instance of a non-unimodal problem. Hence, although not being able to prove the unimodality of the optimization problem, we have strong numerical support that using an admissible risk spectrum is sufficient for the unimodality of the joint inventory & pricing problem with shortage penalty costs.

4.2.2 Joint optimal controls

Again, it is interesting to observe the structural properties of the optimal controls (p^*, y^*) in the joint optimization problem. Looking at the optimal quantity y^* we can observe that for all problem instances a high order quantity can be caused by two reasons. First we observe high order quantities for extreme risk aversion (low values of η). Here the newsvendor is mainly concered with shortage penalty costs, which causes her to place higher orders to avoid them. In the other extreme, when the newsvendor becomes more and more risk-seeking (large η), she increases the order quantity to increase the possibility for high random profit realizations.

In Figure 4.13 we see the optimal quantity y^* for different demand error variabilities, where for this specific set of cost parameters the order quantity is increasing in demand variability. For high ordering cost c the critical ratio $\frac{p^*-c+s}{p^*-v+s}$ decreases so that optimal order quantity can become decreasing in demand variability.

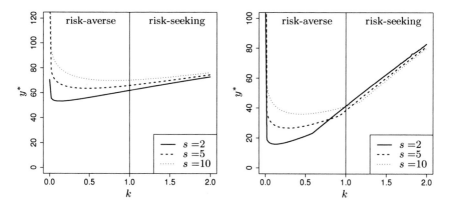

Figure 4.14: Joint optimal y^* for different levels of shortage cost s with additive (left) and multiplicative (right) demand models with a power risk spectrum.

Figure 4.14 illustrates the behaviour of y^* for different shortage penalty costs. While in the additive problem the optimal quantities are ordered with respect to s such that a higher s leads to higher y^*, this relation does not hold for the multiplicative model. The reason behind this is that although the optimal price in the additive model as shown in Figure 4.15 increases in s, the increase is typically very small compared to the multiplicative model. If price stays almost constant, the effect of s is mainly on the quantity, where we know from the inventory-only problem that y^* is increasing in s. For the multiplicative model, however, we see s significantly affecting both quantity and price. For higher levels of η the relative increase in price "overcompensates" the increase in s such that mean demand and optimal order quantity decrease.

Figure 4.16 shows the joint optimal price p^* for different levels of demand variability. A main initial observation is that in the additive model p^* is increasing in η, while for the multiplicative model the opposite behaviour can be true. We can find the same explanation, as we did for the problem without shortage penalty cost. In the additive model the coefficient of variation is increasing in price, hence a risk-averse newsvendor can reduce risk by increasing price. For the multiplicative model, variance is decreasing in price, so the newsvendor will increase price the more risk-averse he is.

Note that for the additive model there are two ranges of η with respect to the ordering of p^* to demand error variability. In the low range an increase in the standard deviation results in a decrease of p^*, while for the high range

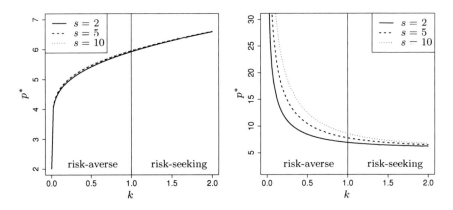

Figure 4.15: Joint optimal p^* for different levels of shortage cost s with additive (left) and multiplicative (right) demand models, power risk spectrum.

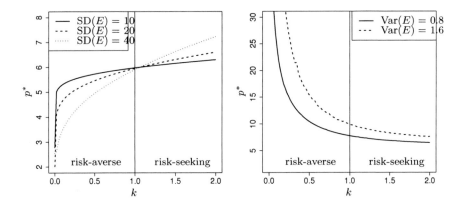

Figure 4.16: Joint optimal p^* for different levels of demand variability with additive (left) and multiplicative (right) demand models, power risk spectrum.

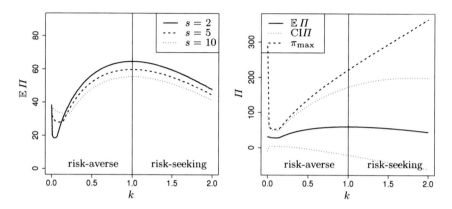

Figure 4.17: Expected profit (left) and confidence intervals of profit (right) for multiplicative demand model, power risk spectrum.

p^* increases. This is an interesting observation as it shows that for any η the newsvendor, to some extent always considers both risk and prospect of the operation. Depending on the parameters, either of the two might dominate and determine the structural behaviour of p^* with respect to variability.

With the same argument as before we can say that if the risk consideration dominates, the newsvendor will decrease price if demand is more variable, as we can see in the example with $k = 0.5$. The newsvendor uses price to compensate for the higher demand variability. If we consider $k = 1.5$, we can see clearly that now the prospect consideration dominates the behaviour. The price is increased to over-proportionally take advantage of variability. We can also say that in the case of small demand error variability, the newsvendor uses price mainly as a tool to optimize the deterministic part of demand, hence the influence of η is rather small. For the case where demand error variability is high enough, price can be more effectively used as a tool to adjust profit variability, and the effect of a change in η on p^* gets stronger. In this case the newsvendor can give up some of the deterministic profit in order to increase the profit made due to the stochastic demand error.

4.2.3 Joint optimal performance measures

Finally, we can analyze the different performance measures as we did in the previous sections. It is obvious that the maximum expected profit is realized for the risk-neutral newsvendor as illustrated in Figure 4.17. However, due to

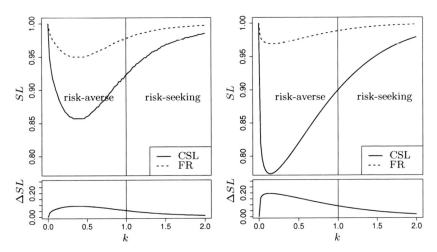

Figure 4.18: Service levels CSL and FR in η for joint optimal (p^*, y^*) for multiplicative (left) with $\mathrm{Var}(E) = 2$ such that $H(\varepsilon)$ is decreasing and additive (right) demand models, power risk spectrum. Under each plot the difference $\Delta SL = FR - CSL$ is shown.

the non-monotonicity of the optimal controls, in particular y^* in η, expected profit for the extremely risk-averse case does not behave monotone in η but increases again as the newsvendor becomes more risk-averse. The decision maker is so obsessed with avoiding shortage penalties that he orders more and as a "by-product" his expected profit increases. We believe that this is an interesting result, that increasing risk aversion might lead to increasing expected profit.

A similar effect can be observed if we look at the service levels in Figure 4.18. Both service levels are increasing in η for wide ranges of η, except for the very risk-averse case. The increasing order quantity for very risk-averse newsvendors also leads to higher service levels. For the internally-oriented probability of missing a profit target we can observe non-monotone behaviour as illustrated in Figure 4.19. In the risk-seeking case, the more risk-seeking the newsvendor becomes the higher the probability of missing a profit target is, since he is willing to accept more risk in order to have the chance of higher profit realizations. As the newsvendor becomes more risk-averse, PL_L is decreasing up to a certain level and increasing again for the very risk-averse cases.

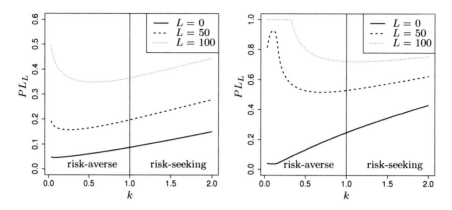

Figure 4.19: Probability of missing a profit target for additive (left) and multiplicative (right) demand models.

Chapter 5

Conclusion

In this work we studied the stochastic single-period, single-item inventory control & pricing problem under spectral measures of risk. The class of spectral risk measures is general in the sense that it can express risk-averse, risk-neutral and risk-seeking risk preferences. It can cover the well-known $CVaR_\alpha$, as well as mean-deviation criteria or continuous risk functions; the power and exponential risk spectra are special cases of spectral risk measures. Using this class of risk measures allows us to generalize structural results obtained so far in the literature.

We divided the problem analysis into two main parts: first we derived optimality conditions and structural results for the inventory-only problem, and in the second part we added price as a decision variable such that we anaylzed a combined inventory & pricing problem. In both parts we considered the situation without and with positive shortage penalty cost separately, as the latter case causes additional technical difficulties.

In the first part of the work, where price is assumed not to affect the demand distribution with zero shortage penalty cost, we were able to prove the concavity of the optimization problem and we could derive simple, closed-form expressions for the optimal order quantity based on a transformation of the demand distribution according to the risk preferences. We were able to show that both the optimal cycle service level and the order quantity increase in the risk preference, meaning that they decrease as the decision maker becomes more risk-averse. This behaviour can be explained by saying that increasing order quantity increases the chance of higher profit realizations, but comes with a higher risk of more leftover inventory. This classical trade-off of the newsvendor model results in different optimal policies since, as risk preferences increase, the decision maker values the chance of higher realizations more than the risk of leftover inventory. An analysis of performance indicators such as expected profit, cycle service level and fill rate as two common service levels and the probability of loss as an internal indicator concluded the inventory problem with zero shortage penalty costs.

The inventory problem with positive shortage penalty costs is technically more demanding. The reason for this is that now random demand and profit realizations are no longer ordered in the same way, since the same low profit realization can be caused either by high leftovers with low demand, or, alternatively, by high shortages with high demand. Because of this the risk measure of profit cannot be written directly in terms of the demand distribution. To overcome this problem either an optimization approach can be used, as proposed by Rockafellar and Uryasev (2002), or in our very specific situation we can take advantage of additional knowledge about profit realizations. As leftovers and shortages are two mutually exclusive events, we were able to sum up their probabilities after some rescaling and rewrite the problem as if there was no shortage penalty cost. Then we were again able to write the problem in terms of the demand distribution and show concavity results for the optimization. Although, in general, an explicit formulation for the optimal order quantity can no longer be found, the problem is reduced to a single-dimensional concave optimization problem for general risk spectra, while the general formulation by Acerbi (2002) results in an optimization problem with an infinite number of degrees of freedom. In the specific case of a piecewise constant risk spectrum we were able to formulate the problem as a system of non-linear equations which can be solved efficiently.

Using a numerical study we were able to conclude that the optimal order quantity is no longer monotone in the risk preference when positive shortage penalty costs must be considered. The explanation for this is that for high risk preferences the newsvendor will order more because he wants to increase the chance for higher profit realizations. On the other hand, as the newsvendor becomes very risk-averse, he is mainly concerned with shortage penalties, as these are generally not bounded from above. As a consequence, he will again increase his order quantity to hedge against the rare high demand events which cause extreme losses.

The second main part of the work was concerned with the combined inventory & pricing problem. Mean demand now depends on price. As is common in the related literature, we used the additive and the multiplicative demand models to combine the deterministic demand with the stochastic error. To ensure unimodality of the joint optimization problem we needed to restrict the risk spectra used to a subset which perserve certain properties. We can show by an example that the mean-$CVaR_\alpha$ risk spectrum does not preserve these properties and may result in multiple local price optima. Instead, the power risk spectrum satisfies all required conditions and turns out to be a flexible model as it can cover risk-averse, risk-neutral and risk-seeking preferences, and is implicitly a mean-deviation formulation already.

A main structural result for the combined problem concerned the price in the risk preference. For the additive model we were able to show that optimal price is increasing in the risk preference, while for the multiplicative model numerical analysis shows that the optimal price is decreasing in the risk preference, under the condition that demand error variability is large enough. This result is particularily interesting as it shows the different strategies used by the newsvendor to hedge against or deal with demand uncertainty, since in the additive model the coefficient of variation of demand increases in price (with constant variance), while the variance decreases in price for the multiplicative model (with constant coefficient of variation).

Considering also shortage penalty costs for the joint problem resulted clearly in the technically most challenging model. In contrast to the previous models, here we were no longer able to derive results analytically; instead, we conducted a numerical study in order to gain insights into this problem. For unimodality of the problem we can numerically identify the same conditions on the distribution functions and risk spectra as for the problem with zero shortage penalty costs. The optimum price in the risk preference is again increasing for the additive and decreasing for the multiplicative demand model, while optimal quantities are non-monotone for both cases. Positive shortage penalty costs also affect the service levels because in the extremely risk-averse case, both measures approach one.

There are plenty of opportunities for further extension of the work. One extension could be with respect to the estimation of the underlying demand model. Typically, linear or log-linear regression is used to estimate the response of demand on price. The commonly used least-squares minimization treats all observations equally so that the regression model might be good on average but for the rather rare outcomes with bad consequences the regression model might not explain demand very well. Hence, similar to applying spectral risk measures, it could be interesting to apply weighted regression for the demand modeling to be able to specifically estimate the lower tails of the demand distribution.

While the current work is strongly based on a normative foundation, a positive study about how good different risk spectra might reflect empirically observeable decision making behaviour could be very helpful. Based on these results the model could be used for supply chain contracting issues, for example where a single manufacturer delivers to multiple risk-averse retailers, where the manufacturer needs to anticipate the response of the retailers on the pricing decision. Furthermore, additional research on technical properties of risk spectra could be done in order to find risk spectra other than $CVaR_\alpha$ and power risk spectrum, where the necessary conditions for the pricing problem are fulfilled.

A challenging task could be the extension of the model to a multi-product setting. Choi and Ruszczyński (2008) and Choi et al. (2009) analyze approximation techniques for quantity optimization when a product portfolio is considered under general law-invariant coherent risk measures. A main conclusion of their work is that the whole product portfolio has to be considered in the optimization when risk measures are applied. To our knowledge, work with respect to the pricing problem in such a setting has not yet been done.

A natural further extension of this work concerns dynamic multi-period models. It would be very interesting to see if, for the inventory-only problem, a basestock policy, or in the inventory & pricing problem, a basestock listprice policy, turns out to be optimal.

References

Acerbi C (2002) Spectral measures of risk: A coherent representation of subjective risk aversion. *Journal of Banking and Finance*, 26(7):1505–1518.

Acerbi C (2004) Coherent representations of subjective risk aversion. In: Szegö G (Ed.), *Risk Measures for the 21st Century*, Wiley.

Acerbi C, Nordio C and Sirton C (2008) Expected shortfall as a tool for financial risk management. Working paper, Abaxbank, Corso Montaforte 34, 20122 Milano, Italy.

Acerbi C and Simonetti P (2002) Portfolio optimization with spectral measures of risk. Working paper, Abaxbank, Corso Montaforte 34, 20122 Milano, Italy.

Agrawal V and Seshadri S (2000) Impact of uncertainty and risk aversion on price and order quantity in the newsvendor problem. *Manufacturing & Service Operations Management*, 2(4):410–423.

Ahmed S, Cakmak U and Shapiro A (2007) Coherent risk measures in inventory problems. *European Journal of Operational Research*, 182:226–238.

Arıkan E, Fichtinger J and Jammernegg W (2007) Single period combined inventory and pricing models. In: Günther HO, Mattfeld D and Suhl L (Eds.), *Management logistischer Netzwerke*, Physica Verlag, pp. 179–199.

Arıkan E and Jammernegg W (2009) The newsvendor problem with a general price dependent demand distribution. Working paper, Vienna University of Economics and Business, available at SSRN: http://ssrn.com/abstract=1523303.

Arrow KJ (1971) *Essays in the theory of risk-bearing*. Markham, Chicago.

Artzner P, Delbaen F, Eber JM and Heath D (1999) Coherent measures of risk. *Mathematical Finance*, 9(3):203–228.

Bamberg G and Coenenberg A (2004) *Betriebswirtschaftliche Entscheidungslehre*. WiSo Kurzlehrbücher, Reihe Betriebswirtschaft, Verlag Vahlen, 12th edn.

Barlow RE and Proschan F (1996) *Mathematical theory of reliability.* Society for Industrial and Applied Mathematics, Philadelphia, USA, 2nd edn.

Bernoulli D (1738) Specimen theoriae novae de mensura sortis. In: *Commentarri Academiae Scientiarum Imperialis Petropolitanae*, Tomus, pp. 175–192, translated by Louise Sommer (1954) as "Expositions of a New Theory on The Measurement of Risk". *Econometrica*, 22:23–26.

Braden DJ and Freimer M (1991) Informational dynamics of censored observations. *Management Science*, 37(11):1390–1404.

Brown AO and Tang CS (2006) The impact of alternative performance measures on single-period inventory policy. *Journal of Industrial and Management Optimization*, 2:297–318.

Cachon GP and Terwiesch C (2006) *Matching supply with demand.* McGraw-Hill.

Chan LMA, Shen ZJM, Simchi-Levi D and Swann JL (2004) Coordination of pricing and inventory decisions: A survey and classification. In: Simchi-Levi D, Wu SD and Shen ZJ (Eds.), *Handbook of Quantitative Supply Chain Analysis – Modeling in the E-Business Era*, chap. 9, Kluwer Academic Publishers, pp. 335–392.

Chen F and Federgruen A (2000) Mean-variance analysis of basic inventory models. Working paper, Graduate School of Business, Columbia University, New York, USA.

Chen X, Shum S and Simchi-Levi D (2008a) Coordinating and rational contracts in supply chains. Working paper, University of Illinois at Urbana-Champaign.

Chen X, Sim M, Simchi-Levi D and Sun P (2004) Risk averse inventory management. Working paper, MIT.

Chen YF, Xu M and Zhang ZG (2008b) A risk-averse newsvendor model under the CVaR criterion. Working paper, Department of System Engineering and Engineering Management, Chinese University of Hong Kong, Shatin, N.T., Hong Kong.

Chen YF, Xu M and Zhang ZG (2009) Technical note – a risk-averse newsvendor model under the CVaR criterion. *Operations Research*, 57(4):1040–1044.

Chen YJ and Seshadri S (2006) Supply chain structure and demand risk. *Automatica*, 42(8):1291–1299.

Choi S and Ruszczyński A (2008) A risk-averse newsvendor with law invariant coherent measures of risk. *Operations Research Letters*, 36:77–82.

Choi S, Ruszczyński A and Zhao Y (2009) A multi-product risk-averse newsvendor with law invariant coherent measures of risk. Working paper, Rutgers University.

Collins RA (2004) The behavior of the risk-averse newsvendor for uniform, truncated normal, negative binomial and gamma distributions of demand. Working paper, Department of Operations and Management Information Systems, Leavey School of Business Santa Clara University, 500 El Camino Real Santa Clara, CA 95053.

Dowd K, Cotter J and Sorwar G (2008) Spectral risk measures: Properties and limitations. *Journal of Financial Services Research*, 34(1):61–75.

Eeckhoudt L, Gollier C and Schlesinger H (1995) The risk-averse (and prudent) newsboy. *Management Science*, 41(5):786–794.

Elmaghraby W and Keskinocak P (2003) Dynamic pricing in the presence of inventory considerations: Research overview, current practices, and future directions. *Management Science*, 49(10):1287–1309.

Fischer K (2004a) *Aspekte einer empirisch fundierten betriebswirtschaftlichen Entscheidungslehre*. Dt. Univ.-Verl, Wiesbaden.

Fischer K (2004b) Value functions versus utility functions. Working paper, Aston Business School, Aston University, Birmingham, UK.

Gan X, Sethi SP and Yan H (2004) Coordination of supply chains with risk-averse agents. *Production and Operations Management*, 13(2):135–149.

Gan X, Sethi SP and Yan H (2005) Channel coordination with a risk-neutral supplier and a downside-risk-averse retailer. *Production and Operations Management*, 14(1):80–89.

Gotoh J and Takano Y (2007) Newsvendor solutions via conditional value-at-risk minimization. *European Journal of Operational Research*, 179:80–96.

Hanisch J (2006) *Risikomessung mit dem Conditional Value-at-Risk*. Verlag Dr. Kovač, Hamburg.

Holton GA (2002) History of value-at-risk: 1922–1998. Working paper, Contingency Analysis, Boston, MA 02199, USA.

Ismail B and Louderback J (1979) Optimizing and satisficing in stochastic cost-volume-profit analysis. *Decision Sciences*, 10(2):205–217.

Jammernegg W and Kischka P (2007) Risk-averse and risk-taking newsvendors: a conditional expected value approach. *Review of Managerial Science*, 1(1):93–110.

Karlin S and Carr CR (1962) Prices and optimal inventory policy. In: Arrow KJ, Karlin S and Scarf H (Eds.), *Studies in Applied Probability and Management Science*, Stanford University Press, CA.

Keren B and Pliskin JS (2006) A benchmark solution for the risk-averse newsvendor problem. *European Journal of Operational Research*, 174(3):1643–1650.

Khouja MJ (1999) The single-period (news-vendor) problem: Literature review and suggestions for future research. *Omega*, 27(5):537–553.

Kocabıyıkoğlu A and Popescu I (2009) An elasticity perspective on the newsvendor with price sensitive demand. Working paper, INSEAD Business School Research Paper No. 2009/13/DS.

Kusuoka S (2001) On law invariant coherent risk measures. *Advanced Mathematical Economics*, 3:83–95.

Lariviere MA (2006) A note on probability distributions with increasing generalized failure rates. *Operations Research*, 54(3):602–604.

Lau HS (1980) The newsboy problem under alternative optimization objectives. *The Journal of the Operational Research Society*, 31(6):525–535.

Lau HS and Lau AHL (1999) Manufacturer's pricing strategy and return policy for a single-period commodity. *European Journal of Operational Research*, 116:291–304.

Laux H (2005) *Entscheidungstheorie*. Springer, Berlin [u.a.], 6th edn.

Levy H (2006) *Stochastic Dominance: Investment Decisions under Uncertainty*. Springer, 2nd edn.

Mao JCT (1970) Models of capital budgeting, E-V vs E-S. *The Journal of Financial and Quantitative Analysis*, 4(5):657–675.

Markowitz H (1952) Portfolio selection. *Journal of Finance*, 7(1):77–91.

Markowitz H (1959) *Portfolio Selection: Efficient diversification of investments*. John Wiley & Sons Inc., 2nd edn, 1991.

Menges G (Ed.) (1974) *Information, inference and decision*. Reidel, Dordrecht.

Mills ES (1959) Uncertainty and price theory. *Quarterly Journal of Economics*, 73:116–130.

Müller A and Stoyan D (2002) *Comparison Methods for Stochastic Models and Risks*. Wiley Series in Probability and Statistics, Wiley, West Sussex, England.

Özler A, Tan B and Karaesmen F (2009) Multi-product newsvendor problem with value-at-risk considerations. *International Journal of Production Economics*, 117(2):244–255.

Petruzzi NC and Dada M (1999) Pricing and the newsvendor problem: A review with extensions. *Operations Research*:183–194.

Pflug GC (2000) Some remarks on the value-at-risk and the conditional value-at-risk. In: Uryasev S (Ed.), *Probabilistic Constrained Optimization*, Nonconvex Optimization and its Applications, Kluwer Academic Publishers.

Pflug GC and Ruszczyński A (2004) A risk measure for income processes. In: Szegö G (Ed.), *Risk Measures for the 21st Century*, Wiley.

Polatoglu L (1991) Optimal order quantity and pricing decisions in single-period inventory systems. *International Journal of Production Economics*, 23(1-3):175–185.

Porteus EL (1990) Stochastic inventory theory. In: Heyman D and Sobel M (Eds.), *Stochastic Models*, vol. 2 of *Handbooks in operations research and management science*, chap. 12, North-Holland, Amsterdam, pp. 605–652.

Pratt JW (1964) Risk aversion in the small and in the large. *Econometrica*, 32:122–136.

R Development Core Team (2010) *R: A Language and Environment for Statistical Computing*. R Foundation for Statistical Computing, Vienna, Austria.

Rockafellar RT and Uryasev S (2000) Optimization of conditional value-at-risk. *Journal of Risk*, 2(3):21–41.

Rockafellar RT and Uryasev S (2002) Conditional value-at-risk for general loss distributions. *Journal of Banking and Finance*, 26(7):1443–1471.

Sarykalin S, Serraino G and Uryasev S (2008) Value-at-risk vs. conditional value-at-risk in risk management and optimization. In: *Tutorials in Operations Research*, INFORMS, pp. 270–294.

Schneeweiß H (1967) *Entscheidungskriterien bei Risiko*. Springer Verlag, Berlin [u.a.].

Schoemaker PJH (1982) The expected utility model: Its variants, purposes, evidence and limitations. *Journal of Economic Literature*, 20:529–563.

Schweitzer ME and Cachon GP (2000) Decision bias in the newsvendor problem with a known demand distribution: Experimental evidence. *Management Science*, 46(3):404–420.

Shi C and Chen B (2007) Pareto-optimal contracts for a supply chain with satisficing objectives. *Journal of the Operational Research Society*, 58(6):751–759.

Shi C, Yang S and Zhao X (2010) Optimal ordering and pricing decisions for a target oriented newsvendor. Working paper, School of Business and Economics, Wilfrid Laurier University, Waterloo, Ontario, Canada.

Sriboonchitta S, Nguyen HT and Kreinovich V (2009) How to relate spectral risk measures and utilities. Working paper, Faculty of Economics, Chiang Mai University, Thailand.

Szegö G (2005) Measures of risk. *European Journal of Operational Research*, 163:5–19.

Tapiero CS (2005) Value at risk and inventory control. *European Journal of Operational Research*, 163(3):769–775.

Tempelmeier H (2005) *Bestandsmanagement in Supply Chains*. Books on Demand, Norderstedt, Germany.

Tomlin B and Wang Y (2005) On the value of mix flexibility and dual sourcing in unreliable newsvendor networks. *Manufacturing & Service Operations Management*, 7(1):37–57.

Topkis DM (1998) *Supermodularity and Complementarity*. Princeton University Books, Princeton, New Jersey, US, 10th edn.

Tsay AA (2002) Risk sensitivity in distribution channel partnerships: implications for manufacturer return policies. *Journal of Retailing*, 78:147–160.

van Mieghem JA (2007) Risk mitigation in newsvendor networks: Resource diversification, flexibility, sharing, and hedging. *Management Science*, 53(8):1269.

von Neumann J and Morgenstern O (1944) *Theory of Games and Economic Behavior*. Princeton University Press, 6th edition, 1990.

Wang CX and Webster S (2007) Channel coordination for a supply chain with a risk-neutral manufacturer and a loss-averse retailer. *Decision Sciences*, 38(3):361–389.

Wang CX and Webster S (2009) The loss-averse newsvendor problem. *Omega*, 37(1):93–105.

Wang CX, Webster S and Suresh NC (2008) Would a risk-averse newsvendor order less at a higher selling price? *European Journal of Operational Research*, in press.

Whitin TM (1955) Inventory control and price theory. *Management Science*, 2(1):61–68.

Wu J, Li J, Wang S and Cheng T (2009) Mean-variance analysis of the newsvendor model with stockout cost. *Omega*, 37:724–730, in press.

Yano CA and Gilbert SM (2004) Coordinated pricing and production/procurement decisions: A review. In: Chakravarty AK and Eliashberg J (Eds.), *Managing Business Interfaces: Marketing, Engineering and Manufacturing Perspectives*, International Series in Quantitative Marketing, chap. 3, Kluwer Academic Publishers, Norwell, Massachusetts, pp. 65–103.

Yao L, Chen YF and Yan H (2006) The newsvendor problem with pricing: Extensions. *International Journal of Management Science and Engineering Management*, 1(1):3–16.

Young L (1978) Price, inventory and the structure of uncertain demand. *New Zealand Operations Research*, 6(2):157–177.

Appendix A

Proofs

Lemma 8. *(See Jammernegg and Kischka, 2007, appendix B) Let F be the continuous, strictly increasing distribution function of demand D. The distribution function of profit, F_Π is*

$$F_\Pi(\pi) = \begin{cases} F\left(\frac{\pi+y(c-v)}{p-v}\right) & \text{for } \pi < (p-c)y \\ 1 & \text{otherwise,} \end{cases} \tag{A.1}$$

so that F_Π is continuous and strictly increasing for $\pi < (p-c)y$. The generalized inverse distribution function of profit, $F_\Pi^{-1}(\omega)$, is then strictly increasing for $\omega \in [0, F(y))$ and $(p-c)y$ for $\omega \in [F(y), 1]$.

Proof. Using the profit formulation as in (1.1), $\Pi(y) = p\min(D, y) - cy + v(y - D)^+$, one can easily see that with a given order quantity y when $D = y$, a maximum possible profit of $(p-c)y$ can be achieved.

Case 1: $\pi > (p-c)y$. For any $D > y$, no further profit improvements can be made. Hence,

$$F_\Pi(\pi) = 1 \quad \text{for } D > y.$$

Case 2: $\pi \le (p-c)y$. For the case $D \le y$, random profit can be written as

$$\Pi = pD - cy + (y - D)v.$$

Exchanging variables,

$$\begin{aligned} F_\Pi(\pi) &= \mathbb{P}(\Pi \le \pi) \\ &= \mathbb{P}(pD - cy + (y - D)v \le \pi) \\ &= \mathbb{P}\left(D \le \frac{\pi + y(c - v)}{p - v}\right) \\ &= F\left(\frac{\pi + y(c - v)}{p - v}\right). \end{aligned}$$

$\square$

Proof of Proposition 4

Since for the problem without penalty cost an ordered relation between demand realizations and profit realizations exists (i. e. the $100\alpha\%$ lowest demand result in the $100\alpha\%$ lowest profit for any α), we can use the definition of the risk measure as in (2.9) directly for the optimization. Hence, we can write the objective function, $M(\Pi(y))$, as

$$M(\Pi(y)) = \int_0^{F(y)} \phi(\omega) F_\Pi^{-1}(\omega) \, d\omega + (p-c)y \int_{F(y)}^1 \phi(\omega) \, d\omega.$$

Let $\Phi(\omega) := \int_0^\omega \phi(u) \, du$, then

$$M(\Pi(y)) = \int_0^{F(y)} \phi(\omega) F_\Pi^{-1}(\omega) \, d\omega + (p-c)y \left(1 - \Phi(F(y))\right),$$

where $F_\Pi^{-1}(\omega)$ for $\omega \in [0, F(y))$ using Lemma 8 is a continuous, monotone increasing function. Hence, we can change the direction of integration and write

$$M(\Pi(y)) = \int_{-(c-v)y}^{(p-c)y} \pi \phi(F_\Pi(\pi)) \, dF_\Pi(\pi) + (p-c)y \left(1 - \Phi(F(y))\right).$$

Replacing profit distribution F_Π with demand distribution F using Lemma 8 leads to the formulation of the risk measure for the newsvendor problem,

$$M(\Pi(y)) = \int_0^y [xp - cy + (y-x)v] \phi(F(x)) \, dF(x) + (p-c)y \left[1 - \Phi(F(y))\right].$$

We are now ready to derive the first order condition to explicitly formulate the optimal order quantity, y^*. Using Leibnitz' rule,

$$\frac{d\,M}{dy} = -(c+v) \int_0^y \phi(F(x)) \, dF(x) + (p-c)[1 - \Phi(F(y))] = 0,$$

Solving for $\Phi(F(y))$,

$$\Phi(F(y)) = \frac{p-c}{p-v}.$$

Note that $\Phi^{-1}(\omega)$ exists for every $\omega \in [0,1]$ since $\phi(\omega)$ is finite by definition.

Finally, we derive the second order condition to show that the optimization problem is concave in y, so

$$\frac{d^2 M}{dy^2} = -(c-v)\phi(F(y))f(y) - (p-c)\phi(F(y))f(y) < 0,$$

since $v < c < p$ and $\phi(\cdot) \geq 0$, $f(\cdot) \geq 0$ by definition. Hence, the problem is a concave maximization problem in y. □

Proof of Lemma 2

Using (1.9) and (1.1) the probability of profit being smaller than a target level L is

$$PL_L = \mathbb{P}(\Pi \leq L) = \mathbb{P}((p-c)y - (p-v)(y-D)^+ \leq L)$$

$$= \mathbb{P}\left(\max(y-D;0) \geq \frac{(p-c)y - L}{p-v}\right)$$

$$= \begin{cases} \mathbb{P}\left(D \leq \frac{(c-v)y+L}{p-v}\right) & \text{for } (p-c)y - L \geq 0 \\ 1 & \text{for } (p-c)y - L < 0 \end{cases}$$

$$= \begin{cases} F\left(\frac{(c-v)y+L}{p-v}\right) & \text{for } (p-c)y - L \geq 0 \\ 1 & \text{for } (p-c)y - L < 0. \end{cases}$$

It can be easily seen that for any $y \geq \frac{L}{p-c}$, PL_L is monotonically increasing in y since F^{-1} is increasing in its argument. □

Proof of Lemma 3

The probability of profit being smaller a certain level, $\mathbb{P}(\Pi \leq \pi)$ is composed of two parts: the event where $D \leq y$ and a second event where $D > y$. Note that these two events are mutually exclusive, therefore for the joint probability we can simply add up the probabilities of the two events. Recall from (3.17),

$$\Pi(y) = \begin{cases} (p-c)D - (c-v)(y-D) & D \leq y \\ (p-c)y - s(D-y) & D > y. \end{cases}$$

Now we can plug in the profit in the distribution function of profit, $F_\Pi(\pi) := \mathbb{P}(\Pi \leq \pi)$, and add up the probabilities of the two exclusive demand events, so that we can express the profit distribution F_Π as a function of the demand distribution F.

$$
\begin{aligned}
F_\Pi(\pi) &= \mathbb{P}\left(\Pi(y) \le \pi,\, D \le y\right) + \mathbb{P}\left(\Pi(y) \le \pi,\, D > y\right) \\
&= \mathbb{P}\left((p-c)D - (c-v)(y-D) \le \pi,\, D \le y\right) \\
&\quad + \mathbb{P}\left((p-c)y - s(D-y) \le \pi,\, D > y\right) \\
&= \mathbb{P}\left(D \le \frac{\pi + (c-v)y}{p-v}\right) + \mathbb{P}\left(D > \frac{(p-c+s)y - \pi}{s}\right) \\
&= F\left(\frac{\pi + (c-v)y}{p-v}\right) + 1 - F\left(\frac{(p-c+s)y - \pi}{s}\right).
\end{aligned}
$$

$\square$

Proof of Proposition 8

Using Acerbi's method easily helps us to show the concavity of $\mathrm{M}(\Pi(y))$ with respect to y. We can formulate the risk measure as in Proposition 3, so

$$
\mathrm{M}(\Pi(y)) = \max_{\psi} \Gamma(y, \psi),
$$

where Γ is defined in (2.14). Since random profit $\Pi(y)$ is concave in y, immediately from Corollary 2 it follows that $\mathrm{M}(\Pi(y))$ is concave in the order quantity.

It remains to derive the risk measure in terms of demand. Since $(p-c)y$ is the maximum possible profit realization for a given y, we can write the risk measure in terms of the profit distribution as

$$
\mathrm{M}(\Pi(y)) = \int_{-\infty}^{(p-c)y} t \, d\Phi(F_\Pi(t)).
$$

Exchanging the variable of integration t over profits by demand x, it follows that

$$
\begin{aligned}
\mathrm{M}(\Pi(y)) &= \int_{-\infty}^{y} \pi(x, y) \, d\Phi(G(x)) \\
&= \int_{-\infty}^{y} ((p-v)x - (c-v)y)\left(f(x) + f(\bar{x})\frac{p-v}{s}\right) \phi\left(F(x) + 1 - F(\bar{x})\right) dx.
\end{aligned}
$$

Using integration by parts,

$$M(\Pi(y)) = (p - c)y - (p - v)\int_{-\infty}^{y}\Phi\Big(F(x) + 1 - F(\bar{x})\Big)\,dx.$$

$\square$

Proof of Lemma 4

Recall that for a CVaR$_\alpha$ decision maker $\phi = \frac{1}{\alpha}$ for $0 \le \omega \le \alpha$ and 0 otherwise. Now, let $x^o < y$ be the demand up to which the corresponding profits are considered by having positive weights, so where $\phi(F_\Pi) = \frac{1}{\alpha}$. The corresponding demand level larger y, i.e. $\bar{x}^o$, can be derived as shown in (3.18), so

$$\bar{x}^o = y + (y - x^o)\frac{p - v}{s}.$$

Hence, x^o should satisfy

$$G(x^o) = F(x^o) + 1 - F(\bar{x}^o) = \alpha. \tag{A.2}$$

Since $\bar{x}^o$ depends on y, when y changes also x^o should change so that (A.2) is satisfied again. Thus x^o is implicitly a function of y. Now we can define $x^{o\prime} = \frac{dx^o}{dy}$ and $\bar{x}^{o\prime} = \frac{d\bar{x}^o}{dy}$, taking the derivative of (A.2) with respect to y leads to

$$x^{o\prime}f(x^o) - \bar{x}^{o\prime}f(\bar{x}^o) = 0. \tag{A.3}$$

Based on the general formulation of M(Π) in (3.23) we can write

$$M(\Pi(y)) = \frac{1}{\alpha}\int_{-\infty}^{x^o}((p - c)x - (c - v)(y - x))f(\bar{x})\frac{p - v}{s}\,dx$$

$$+ \frac{1}{\alpha}\int_{-\infty}^{x^o}((p - c)x - (c - v)(y - x))f(x)\,dx.$$

Substituting $\bar{x}$ for x in the first integral leads to

$$M(\Pi(y)) = \frac{1}{\alpha}\int_{\bar{x}^o}^{\infty}((p - c)y - s(\bar{x} - y))f(\bar{x})\,d\bar{x}$$

$$+ \frac{1}{\alpha}\int_{-\infty}^{x^o}((p - c)x - (c - v)(y - x))f(x)\,dx,$$

taking the derivative with respect to y using (A.3),

$$M'(\Pi(y)) = \frac{1}{\alpha}\Big((p - c + s)(1 - F(\bar{x}^o)) - (c - v)F(x^o)\Big).$$

Using (A.2) we can solve this for

$$F(x^{o*}) = \alpha\frac{p - c + s}{p - v + s}, \quad F(\bar{x}^{o*}) = 1 - \alpha\frac{c - v}{p - v + s},$$

and

$$y^* = \frac{p - v}{p - v + s}F^{-1}\Big(\alpha\frac{p - c + s}{p - v + s}\Big) + \frac{s}{p - v + s}F^{-1}\Big(1 - \alpha\frac{c - v}{p - v + s}\Big).$$

$\square$

Proof of Lemma 6

Following the same line of argument as in the proof of Corollary 4, we now define J demand levels as

$$\bar{x}_i^o = y + (y - x_i^o)\frac{p - v}{s} \quad \text{for all } i = 1\ldots J,$$

and $x_0^o := -\infty$ and $x_{J+1}^o := y$, so $\bar{x}_0^o = \infty$ and $x_{J+1}^o = y$ which satisfy

$$F(x_i^o) + 1 - F(\bar{x}_i^o) = w_i \quad \text{for all } i = 1\ldots J.$$

The risk measure can be formulated as

$$M(\Pi(y)) = \sum_{i=1}^{J+1} \phi_i\Bigg[\int_{\bar{x}_i^o}^{\bar{x}_{i-1}^o} ((p - c)y - s(\bar{x} - y))f(\bar{x})\,d\bar{x}$$
$$+ \int_{x_{i-1}^o}^{x_i^o} ((p - c)x - (c - v)(y - x))f(x)\,dx\Bigg].$$

Taking derivatives leads to the first order condition as the system of equations

$$\frac{d\,\mathrm{M}(\Pi(y))}{dy} = \sum_{i=1}^{J+1} \phi_i \left[(p - c + s)\Big(F(\bar{x}_{i-1}^o) - F(\bar{x}_i^o)\Big) \right.$$

$$\left. - (c - v)\Big(F(x_i^o) - F(x_{i-1}^o)\Big) \right] = 0,$$

$$F(x_i^o) + 1 - F(\bar{x}_i^o) = \omega_i \quad \text{for all } i.$$

$\square$

Proof of Proposition 11

For the additive model, we write the objective function as

$$\mathrm{M}(\Pi(p, z^*(p))) = \mathrm{M}(\Pi(p)) = (p-c)d(p)+(p-c)z^*(p)-(p-v)\int_{-\infty}^{z^*(p)} F_\phi(\varepsilon)\,d\varepsilon,$$

with cross derivative

$$\frac{\partial^2 \,\mathrm{M}(\Pi(p))}{\partial v \partial p} = \frac{dz^*(p)}{dv}\left(1 - \frac{p-c}{p-v}\right) > 0.$$

The second term is positive by definition since $p \geq c \geq v$. To see that $z^*(p)$ is increasing in v, we take the derivative with respect to v from $F_\phi(z^*(p)) = \frac{p-c}{p-v}$,

$$\frac{dz^*(p)}{dv} = \frac{1}{f_\phi(z^*(p))}\frac{p-c}{(p-v)^2} > 0.$$

Hence, the risk measure of profit is supermodular in (p^*, v), so p^* is increasing in v. $\square$

Proof of Proposition 12

We write the objective function in terms of the degree of risk aversion, η using the optimal stocking factor $z^*(p)$. Note that the risk-transformed distribution function $F_\phi(\varepsilon)$ changes with η. Let us first show part (a) for the *additive model.*

$$M(\Pi(p, z^*(p))) = M(\Pi(p)) = (p-c)(d(p) + z^*(p)) - (p-v) \int_{-\infty}^{z^*(p)} F_\phi(\varepsilon) \, d\varepsilon.$$

The cross derivative is

$$\frac{\partial^2 M(\Pi(p))}{\partial\eta\partial p} = \frac{\partial z^*(p)}{\partial\eta} (1 - F_\phi(z^*(p))) - \int_{-\infty}^{z^*(p)} \frac{\partial F_\phi(\varepsilon)}{\partial\eta} \, d\varepsilon, \qquad (A.4)$$

where $F_\phi(z^*(p)) = \frac{p-c}{p-v}$. By Definition 6(b), $\Phi(\omega)$ decreases in η, hence also $F_\phi(\varepsilon) = \Phi(F(\varepsilon))$ decreases in η. Furthermore, the optimal $z^*(p) = F_\phi^{-1}\left(\frac{p-c}{p-v}\right)$ for a given p increases in η. Hence, since $0 \le F_\phi(z^*(p)) \le 1$ the first term in (A.4) is positive, while the second term is negative so that the whole expression is positive. This is sufficient for $M(\Pi(p))$ being supermodular in (p^*, η) and p^* being increasing in η.

Now we can show part (b) for the *multiplicative model.* The first derivative with respect to price is

$$\frac{\partial M(\Pi(p))}{\partial p}\bigg|_{p=p^*} = d'(p^*) \left[p^* \int_0^{z^*(p^*)} (1 - F_\phi(\varepsilon)) \, d\varepsilon - cz^*(p^*) \right]$$
$$+ d(p^*) \int_0^{z^*(p^*)} (1 - F_\phi(\varepsilon)) \, d\varepsilon = 0,$$

hence

$$d'(p^*) = -\frac{d(p^*) \int_0^{z^*(p^*)} (1 - F_\phi(\varepsilon)) \, d\varepsilon}{p^* \int_0^{z^*(p^*)} (1 - F_\phi(\varepsilon)) \, d\varepsilon - cz^*(p^*)}.$$

Recall that $\epsilon(p)$ denotes the price elasticity,

$$\epsilon(p^*) = -\frac{p^* d'(p)}{d(p^*)} = p^* \frac{\int_0^{z^*(p^*)} (1 - F_\phi(\varepsilon)) \, d\varepsilon}{p^* \int_0^{z^*(p^*)} (1 - F_\phi(\varepsilon)) \, d\varepsilon - cz^*(p^*)}, \text{ and}$$

$$1 - \epsilon(p^*) = \frac{d(p^*) - p^* d'(p^*)}{d(p^*)} = \frac{-cz^*(p^*)}{p^* \int_0^{z^*(p^*)} (1 - F_\phi(\varepsilon)) \, d\varepsilon - cz^*(p^*)}. \qquad (A.5)$$

Using integration by parts, we can rewrite the denominator as

$$1 - \epsilon(p^*) = \frac{-cz^*(p^*)}{p^* \int_0^{z^*(p^*)} \varepsilon f_\phi(\varepsilon)\, d\varepsilon}. \tag{A.6}$$

The cross derivative is

$$\frac{\partial^2 \mathrm{M}(\Pi(p))}{\partial\eta\partial p} =$$

$$= d'(p)\left[-p\int_0^{z^*(p)} \frac{\partial F_\phi(\varepsilon)}{\partial\eta}\, d\varepsilon + p\frac{\partial z^*(p)}{\partial\eta}(1 - F_\phi(z^*(p))) - cz^*(p) \right]$$

$$+ d(p)\left[-\int_0^{z^*(p)} \frac{\partial F_\phi(\varepsilon)}{\partial\eta}(\varepsilon)\, d\varepsilon + \frac{\partial z^*(p)}{\partial\eta}(1 - F_\phi(z^*(p))) \right],$$

where $F_\phi(z^*(p)) = \frac{p-c}{p}$, so

$$\frac{\partial^2 \mathrm{M}(\Pi(p))}{\partial\eta\partial p} = -\int_0^{z^*(p)} \frac{\partial F_\phi(\varepsilon)}{\partial\eta}\, d\varepsilon \cdot \Big(d(p) + pd'(p) \Big) + d(p)\frac{\partial z^*(p)}{\partial\eta}\frac{c}{p}$$

Since $d(p^*) + p^*d'(p^*) = d(p^*)(1 - \epsilon(p^*))$ from (A.5), we can write

$$\left. \frac{\partial^2 \mathrm{M}(\Pi(p))}{\partial\eta\partial p} \right|_{p=p^*} =$$

$$= d(p^*)\left[-(1 - \epsilon(p^*))\int_0^{z^*(p^*)} \frac{\partial F_\phi(\varepsilon)}{\partial\eta}\, d\varepsilon + \left.\frac{\partial z^*(p)}{\partial\eta}\right|_{p^*} \cdot \frac{c}{p^*} \right].$$

Plugging in (A.6),

$$
\frac{\partial^2 \, \mathrm{M}(\Pi(p))}{\partial \eta \partial p}\bigg|_{p=p^*} = d(p^*) \left[\frac{c}{p^*} \frac{z^*(p^*) \displaystyle\int_0^{z^*(p^*)} \frac{\partial F_\phi(\varepsilon)}{\partial \eta} \, d\varepsilon}{\displaystyle\int_0^{z^*(p^*)} \varepsilon f_\phi(\varepsilon) \, d\varepsilon} + \frac{\partial z^*(p)}{\partial \eta}\bigg|_{p^*} \cdot \frac{c}{p^*} \right]
$$

$$
= d(p^*) \frac{c}{p^*} \left[\frac{z^*(p^*) \displaystyle\int_0^{z^*(p^*)} \frac{\partial F_\phi(\varepsilon)}{\partial \eta} \, d\varepsilon + \frac{\partial z^*(p)}{\partial \eta}\bigg|_{p^*} \cdot \displaystyle\int_0^{z^*(p^*)} \varepsilon f_\phi(\varepsilon) \, d\varepsilon}{\displaystyle\int_0^{z^*(p^*)} \varepsilon f_\phi(\varepsilon) \, d\varepsilon} \right].
$$

Since

$$
\frac{\partial z^*(p)}{\partial \eta} = - \frac{\partial F_\phi(\varepsilon)}{\partial \eta}\bigg|_{\varepsilon = z^*(p)} \times \frac{1}{f_\phi(z^*(p))},
$$

we can write

$$
\frac{\partial^2 \, \mathrm{M}(\Pi(p))}{\partial \eta \partial p}\bigg|_{p=p^*} = d(p^*) \frac{c}{p^*} \left(\int_0^{z^*(p^*)} \varepsilon f_\phi(\varepsilon) \, d\varepsilon \right)^{-1} \frac{1}{f_\phi(z^*(p^*))}
$$

$$
\times \left[z^*(p^*) f_\phi(z^*(p^*)) \int_0^{z^*(p^*)} \frac{\partial F_\phi(\varepsilon)}{\partial \eta} \, d\varepsilon \right.
$$

$$
\left. - \frac{\partial G(z^*(p^*))}{\partial \eta} \int_0^{z^*(p^*)} \varepsilon f_\phi(\varepsilon) \, d\varepsilon \right],
$$

where the first terms are all positive and the expression in $[\,\cdot\,]$ can be written as

$$
\int_0^{z^*(p^*)} \frac{\partial F_\phi(\varepsilon)}{\partial \eta} \frac{\partial F_\phi(z^*(p^*))}{\partial \eta} \left\{ \frac{z^*(p^*) f_\phi(z^*(p^*))}{\frac{\partial F_\phi(z^*(p^*))}{\partial \eta}} - \frac{\varepsilon f_\phi(\varepsilon)}{\frac{\partial F_\phi(\varepsilon)}{\partial \eta}} \right\} \, d\varepsilon. \tag{A.7}
$$

This expression is positive if

$$
\frac{d}{dx} \left(\frac{x f_\phi(x)}{\frac{\partial}{\partial \eta} F_\phi(x)} \right) > 0,
$$

so if the second fraction in (A.7) is increasing in ε. $\square$

Proof of Proposition 13

Let us first show the monotonicity of $p^*(y)$ for an *additive demand model*. Note that for ease of expression we show the derivations without considering salvage value, so $v = 0$. It can be easily extended to $v > 0$. We can write

$$M(\Pi(p,y)) = \int_{-d(p)}^{y-d(p)} p(d(p) + \varepsilon)f_\phi(\varepsilon) d\varepsilon + \int_{y-d(p)}^{\infty} pyf_\phi(\varepsilon) d\varepsilon - cy.$$

Using $y = d(p) + z$,

$$M(\Pi(p,y)) = (p - c)y - p \int_{-d(p)}^{y-d(p)} (z - \varepsilon)f_\phi(\varepsilon) d\varepsilon.$$

Using integration by parts,

$$M(\Pi(p,y)) = (p - c)y - p \int_{-d(p)}^{y-d(p)} F_\phi(\varepsilon) d\varepsilon.$$

The first order condition for optimal $p^*(y)$ is then

$$\left.\frac{\partial M(\Pi(p,y))}{\partial p}\right|_{p=p^*(y)} = \left.\int_{-d(p)}^{y-d(p)} [1 - F_\phi(\varepsilon) + pd'(p)f_\phi(\varepsilon)] d\varepsilon\right|_{p=p^*(y)} = 0.$$

$$(A.8)$$

Note that $F_\phi(-d(p)) = 0$. Using the implicit function theorem,

$$\frac{dp^*(y)}{dy} = -\left.\frac{\partial^2 M(\Pi(p,y))}{\partial y \partial p} \left(\frac{\partial^2 M(\Pi(p,y))}{\partial p^2}\right)^{-1}\right|_{p=p^*(y)},$$

where the second term is negative because of the second order condition for optimality of $p^*(y)$. For a decreasing $p^*(y)$ it remains to show that the first term is negative. It can be written as

$$\frac{\partial^2 M(\Pi(p,y))}{\partial y \partial p} = 1 - F_\phi(y - d(p)) + pd'(p)f_\phi(y - d(p)) \qquad (A.9)$$

Now, let $R(p,\varepsilon) := -pd'(p)\frac{f_\phi(\varepsilon)}{1-F_\phi(\varepsilon)}$ so that

$$1 - F_\phi(\varepsilon) + pd'(p)f_\phi(\varepsilon) = (1 - F_\phi(\varepsilon))(1 - R(p,\varepsilon)).$$

Now we show that for $p = p^*(y)$, (A.9) is negative by contradiction. Assume

$$(1 - F_\phi(\varepsilon))(1 - R(p, \varepsilon))\big|_{\varepsilon = y - d(p)} \geq 0.$$

Because $(1 - F_\phi(\cdot)) \geq 0$ it follows that $1 - R(p, \varepsilon)\big|_{\varepsilon = y - d(p)} \geq 0$. $R(p, \varepsilon)$ is increasing in ε, since F has IFR and the risk spectrum preserves the IFR property, which implies that $\frac{f_\phi(\varepsilon)}{1 - F_\phi(\varepsilon)}$ is increasing in ε. Hence, $1 - R(p, \varepsilon) > 0$ for any $\varepsilon \in (-d(p), y - d(p))$. It follows that

$$\int_{-d(p)}^{y - d(p)} (1 - F_\phi(p, \varepsilon))(1 - R(p, \varepsilon)) \, d\varepsilon \bigg|_{p = p^*(y)} > 0,$$

which is a contradiction to (A.8).

The proof for the *multiplicative demand function* is very similar. The cross derivative is

$$\frac{\partial^2 \operatorname{M}(\Pi(p, y))}{\partial y \partial p} = 1 - F_\phi\left(\frac{y}{d(p)}\right) + \frac{pd'(p)}{d(p)} \frac{y}{d(p)} f_\phi\left(\frac{y}{d(p)}\right). \tag{A.10}$$

We can define $R(p, \varepsilon) := \frac{pd'(p)}{d(p)} \frac{\varepsilon f_\phi(\varepsilon)}{1 - F_\phi(\varepsilon)}$ which is increasing in ε. Using the same argument by contradiction as before, $(1 - F_\phi(\varepsilon))(1 - R(p, \varepsilon))\big|_{\varepsilon = \frac{y}{d(p)}} < 0$, which implies that (A.10) is negative for $p = p^*(y)$ and $p^*(y)$ is decreasing in y. □

Proof of Corollary 6

It is easy to see that the risk measure of the profit from the demand error,

$$\operatorname{M}(\Pi_\varepsilon(p, z)) = (p - c)z - (p - v) \int_{-\infty}^{z} F_\phi(\varepsilon) \, d\varepsilon,$$

is supermodular in (p, z), since

$$\frac{\partial^2 \operatorname{M}(\Pi_\varepsilon(p, z))}{\partial z \partial p} = 1 - F_\phi(z) > 0.$$

Hence, independent of the underlying demand model p^* is increasing in z. □

Proof of Corollary 7

Let us first show the behaviour for the *additive demand* model. We write the risk measure of profit as a function of p and η,

$$\mathrm{M}(\Pi(p, z)) = (p - c)(d(p) + z) - (p - v) \int_{-\infty}^{z} F_{\phi}(\varepsilon)\, d\varepsilon,$$

with cross derivative,

$$\frac{\partial^2 \mathrm{M}(\Pi(p, z))}{\partial p \partial \eta} = - \int_{-\infty}^{z} \frac{\partial}{\partial \eta} F_{\phi}(\varepsilon)\, d\varepsilon > 0.$$

This holds since by Definition 6(b) F_{ϕ} is decreasing in η. Hence, the risk measure is supermodular in (p^*, η) for a given z and $p^*(z)$ is increasing in η.

Now we can show the behavior for the *multiplicative demand* model. Here the risk measure of profit is

$$\mathrm{M}(\Pi(p, z)) = d(p) \left[(p - c)z - (p - v) \int_{0}^{z} F_{\phi}(\varepsilon)\, d\varepsilon \right],$$

with cross derivative

$$\frac{\partial^2 \mathrm{M}(\Pi(p, z))}{\partial p \partial \eta} = - \Big(d'(p)(p - v) + d(p) \Big) \int_{0}^{z} \frac{\partial}{\partial \eta} F_{\phi}(\varepsilon)\, d\varepsilon. \qquad (\mathrm{A}.11)$$

The integral is with negative the same reasoning as before in the additive model. What remains, is to show that the first term is negative. The first order condition for optimality of price is

$$\frac{\partial \mathrm{M}(\Pi(p, z))}{\partial p} = - \Big(d'(p)(p - v) + d(p) \Big)$$

$$\times \int_{0}^{z} F_{\phi}(\varepsilon)\, d\varepsilon + z \Big(d'(p)(p - c) + d(p) \Big) \Bigg|_{p = p^*(z)} = 0.$$

Since $p - c < p - v$, we can write

$$\Big(d'(p)(p - v) + d(p) \Big) \left(z - \int_{0}^{z} F_{\phi}(\varepsilon)\, d\varepsilon \right) < 0.$$

Since $F_\phi(\cdot) \leq 1$, the integral is smaller than z and the right term is positive. Hence, the first term is negative, so that also (A.11) is negative. The problem is submodular in (p^*, η), so $p^*(z)$ is decreasing in η. $\qquad\square$

Forschungsergebnisse der Wirtschaftsuniversität Wien

Herausgeber: Wirtschaftsuniversität Wien –
vertreten durch a.o. Univ. Prof. Dr. Barbara Sporn

INFORMATION UND KONTAKT:

WU (Wirtschaftsuniversität Wien)
Department of Finance, Accounting and Statistics
Institute for Finance, Banking and Insurance
Heiligenstädter Straße 46-48, 1190 Wien
Tel.: 0043-1-313 36/4556
Fax: 0043-1-313 36/904556
valentine.wendling@wu.ac.at
www.wu.ac.at/finance

Band 16 Markus Imgrund: Wege aus der Insolvenz. Eine Analyse der Fortführung und Sanierung insolventer Klein- und Mittelbetriebe unter besonderer Berücksichtigung des Konfigurationsansatzes. 2007.

Band 17 Nicolas Knotzer: Product Recommendations in E-Commerce Retailing Applications. 2008.

Band 18 Astrid Dickinger: Perceived Quality of Mobile Services. A Segment-Specific Analysis. 2007.

Band 19 Nadine Wiedermann-Ondrej: Hybride Finanzierungsinstrumente in der nationalen und internationalen Besteuerung der USA. 2008.

Band 20 Helmut Sorger: Entscheidungsorientiertes Risikomanagement in der Industrieunternehmung. 2008.

Band 21 Martin Rietsch: Messung und Analyse des ökonomischen Wechselkursrisikos aus Unternehmenssicht: Ein stochastischer Simulationsansatz. 2008.

Band 22 Hans Christian Mantler: Makroökonomische Effizienz des Finanzsektors. Herleitung eines theoretischen Modells und Schätzung der Wachstumsimplikationen für die Marktwirtschaften und Transformationsökonomien Europas. 2008.

Band 23 Youri Tacoun: La théorie de la valeur de Christian von Ehrenfels. 2008.

Band 24 Monika Koller: Longitudinale Betrachtung der Kognitiven Dissonanz. Eine Tagebuchstudie zur Reiseentscheidung. 2008.

Band 25 Marcus Scheiblecker: The Austrian Business Cycle in the European Context. 2008.

Band 26 Aida Numic: Multinational Teams in European and American Companies. 2008.

Band 27 Ulrike Bauernfeind: User Satisfaction with Personalised Internet Applications. 2008.

Band 28 Reinhold Schodl: Systematische Analyse und Bewertung komplexer Supply Chain Prozesse bei dynamischer Festlegung des Auftragsentkopplungspunkts. 2008.

Band 29 Bianca Gusenbauer: Öffentlich-private Finanzierung von Infrastruktur in Entwicklungsländern und deren Beitrag zur Armutsreduktion. Fallstudien in Vietnam und auf den Philippinen. 2009.

Band 30 Elisabeth Salomon: Hybrides Management in sino-österreichischen Joint Ventures in China aus österreichischer Perspektive. 2009.

Band 31 Katharina Mader: Gender Budgeting: Ein emanzipatorisches, finanzpolitisches und demokratiepolitisches Instrument. 2009.

Band 32 Michael Weber: Die Generierung von Empfehlungen für zwischenbetriebliche Transaktionen als gesamtwirtschaftliche Infrastrukturleistung. 2010.

Band 33 Lisa Gimpl-Heersink: Joint Pricing and Inventory Control under Reference Price Effects. 2009.

Band 34 Erscheint nicht.

Band 35 Dagmar Kiefer: Multicultural Work in Five United Nations Organisations. An Austrian Perspective. 2009.

Band 36 Gottfried Gruber: Multichannel Management. A Normative Model Towards Optimality. 2009.

Band 37 Rainer Quante: Management of Stochastic Demand in Make-to-Stock Manufacturing. 2009.

Band 38 Franz F. Eiffe: Auf den Spuren von Amartya Sen. Zur theoriegeschichtlichen Genese des Capability-Ansatzes und seinem Beitrag zur Armutsanalyse in der EU. 2010.

www.peterlang.de

Emel Arikan

Single Period Inventory Control and Pricing

An Empirical and Analytical Study of a Generalized Model

Frankfurt am Main, Berlin, Bern, Bruxelles, New York, Oxford, Wien, 2011.
115 pp., 13 tab., 28 graph.
Forschungsergebnisse der Wirtschaftsuniversität Wien.
Edited by Barbara Sporn. Vol. 43
ISBN 978-3-631-61222-4 · hb. € 24,80*

The price-setting newsvendor model is used to address the single period joint pricing and inventory control problem. The objective is to set the optimal price and replenishment quantity of a single product in order to maximize the expected profit. Products with a short selling season and relatively long replenishment lead times such as fashion goods are the most relevant application areas of the model. The focus of the work is the generalization of the model with respect to the modeling of uncertainty in demand. The author presents an analytical and empirical study which compares different demand models with a more flexible model based on price and inventory optimization. She concludes that using a general model can increase the profits significantly.

Content: Inventory management · Review of the newsvendor model · Price-taking and price-setting newsvendor model · Empirical study · Simulation of profits · Analysis of the generalized model · Elasticity of expected sales · Optimality conditions · Structural properties · Numerical study

Peter Lang · Internationaler Verlag der Wissenschaften

Frankfurt am Main · Berlin · Bern · Bruxelles · New York · Oxford · Wien
Distribution: Verlag Peter Lang AG
Moosstr. 1, CH-2542 Pieterlen
Telefax 00 41 (0) 32 / 376 17 27

*The €-price includes German tax rate
Prices are subject to change without notice
Homepage http://www.peterlang.de